AWESOME KYIV

Interesting things you need to know

4th edition

Kyiv
Osnovy Publishing
2019

GENESIS

Genesis is one of the largest IT companies in Ukraine with 1500 people in 9 different countries.

The company leverages extensive experience in developing high loaded platforms and utilizes adept knowledge in user acquisition to host over 150 million unique visitors per month on projects worldwide.

Genesis' global technology reach includes operations in North America and Europe as well as expansion into emerging markets within Asia and Africa.

Genesis is one of the largest partners of big companies-giants as Facebook, Google, Snapchat and Apple in the CEE region.

By partnering with preeminent entrepreneurs in Ukraine, we create leading global technologies that empower and enrich the lives of millions.

УДК 908(477)(03)=111
Ц60

Authors of Awesome Ukraine Series — Hanna Kopylova, Dana Pavlychko
Executive Editor — Nadia Chervinska
Authors of texts — Igor Makhtiienko, Viktoria Linchevskaya
English Editor — Daisy Gibbons
Editorial Assistant — Anastasia Mishustina
Cover illustration — Zukentiy Gorobiyov
Design and layout — Dmytro Ermolov, Dmytro Denyschyk
Photo Editor — Anna Lysiuk

Osnovy Publishing
ilovebooks@osnovypublishing.com
www.osnovypublishing.com

Printing — Publish Pro
www.publishpro.com.ua

ISBN 978-966-500-841-5

Foreword

Kyiv is intoxicating. The city explodes with art and culture. Across Kyiv's numerous squares, locals debate politics, play chess and gossip. Its layered history, lush parks and hidden islands along the wide Dnipro provide for endless exploration. Its tree-lined promenades entice lovers to stroll and revelers to gawk. It's a city of flaneurs. Of poets. Of politics.

With this book we are pleased to share with you our love of Kyiv! The book is neither a guide nor a manual. Rather, it's an insight into the city we adore — wonderful, fascinating and strange.

In its pages you'll find references to major historical events, famous and talented residents, art, culture, sports, literature, traditions and even beloved street food.

Contents

HISTORY

CULTURE

FOOD

PLACES

HISTORY

1 Kyi, Shchek, Khoryv and Lybid
2 Volodymyr the Great
3 Yaroslav the Wise
4 Anna Yaroslavna
5 Magdeburg Rights
6 Ivan Mazepa
7 Kyiv Governorate
8 Mykhailo Hrushevskyi
9 Babyn Yar
10 Independence Day
11 Orange Revolution
12 Euromaidan

Right page: Sasha Kurmaz, ***Molotov cocktail****, 2014*

THE ORIGINAL QUALITY

1

Kyi, Shchek, Khoryv and Lybid

Kyiv was founded by three brothers — Kyi the warrior, Shchek the tiller, Khoryv the hunter — and their sister Lybid

The early history of Kyiv was chronicled by the aptly named Saint Nestor the Chronicler — a monk who lived in the Monastery Caves in Kyiv in the tenth-eleventh centuries. Nestor's Primary Chronicle tells of three Polian princes — Kyi, Shchek and Khoryv — who, together with their sister Lybid, founded a city on the picturesque banks of the Dnipro River in the sixth century. While it is the elder brother's name that has been immortalized in the name of the city, the names of the other founders also feature in the city's modern toponymy.

For example, Shchekavytsia Mountainis named after Shchek. The mountain (more of a hill, really) is home to ancient burial sites. It's a perfect place to step off Kyiv's bustling streets and drink in the view of St. Andrew's Church and Podil below. Khoryv also had a mountain named after him, though researchers disagree on its exact location; some think it is Zamkova Mountain, others favor Yurkovytsia. But there is no doubt as

The monument to Kyiv's founders sits on the embankment of the Dnipro. It's ***a popular location for wedding photographs***

Kyi, Shchek, Khoryv and Lybid are featured in ***the Radzywill Chronicle*** — an illustrated manuscript dating back to the fifteenth century

Left page: A fresco with the image of Kyi, Shchek, Khoryv and Lybid at the Golden Gate Metro station

to where Khoryv Street is located — it is one of the most ancient streets in Kyiv. Nestled in the Podil District, Khoryv Street has a number of architectural landmarks from the middle and late nineteenth century, and is home to the church of Mykola Prytysk, built in the Ukrainian Baroque style.

The name of the youngest of the siblings, the sister, was given to the river Lybid. In the nineteenth century this right tributary of the Dnipro was navigable, and city dwellers would fish there for tasty crucian carps and breams. Sadly, with growing urbanization, the river became polluted and the city authorities ended up hiding the Lybid in an underground sewer. Perhaps it's time to rectify this — to open the river up, reviving it and Lybid's name in the process.

2

Volodymyr the Great

In the year 988, Prince Volodymyr I Svyatoslavych turned the pagan Kyivan Rus into a Christian state

Volodymyr was the youngest (and extramarital) son of the Grand Prince of Kyiv, Svyatoslav Ihorevich and Malusha, the housekeeper of Princess Olga.

When Svyatoslav died, his various sons fell into a power struggle for the lands of Kyiv. Volodymyr managed to rally considerable forces, and with the help of hired Norse mercenaries he emerged victorious.

Upon assuming the throne in 980, Volodymyr launched a number of reforms. Religious reform was chief among them. The prince recognized the increasing prevalence of monotheism over paganism in many countries. After marrying Anna, a Byzantine princess, Volodymyr adopted Christianity and baptized his people. The solemn baptism of Kyivans

A monument to Volodymyr was constructed on the banks of the Dnipro in 1853. In 1895, local donors raised funds to provide the monument with electrical lighting. During Soviet times the lighting was removed, only to be installed once again upon Ukraine's Independence

Volodymyr's portrait can be found on modern banknotes and coins worth ***one hryvnia***

Left page: Volodymyr's image on a Kyivian Rus coin
*Top: **The Baptism of Rus**, a fresco by Viktor Vasnetsov*

took place in 988, on the banks of the Dnipro.

The first stone church in Kyivan Rus — Desiatynna — became the symbol of the new faith. Volodymyr allocated one tenth of his income for its construction. The church was ruined in 1240 by the horde of Batu Khan, but the building's foundation survives to the present day. Under this church, Volodymyr opened the country's first school of "book learning" and actively supported the development of written language.

3

Yaroslav the Wise

Yaroslav the Wise's rule ushered in the high noon of cultural and spiritual life in Kyivan Rus

Yaroslav the Wise was the son of Prince Volodymyr the Great and the Cuman Princess Rognida. He was born lame, and compensated for his physical limitations with an unquenchable thirst for knowledge. Shrewd and ambitious, he became ruler of Novgorod and rebelled against his father, refusing to pay him tribute. Volodymyr's death resolved this conflict, but soon Yaroslav and his brother, Sviatopolk, engaged in a fierce battle for the throne. Yaroslav was victorious and became the great prince of Kyiv in 1019.

Why was he considered wise? Well, beyond his love of learning, he pursued a number of important legislative reforms and built significant monuments. In the first years of his rule, the prince began to standardize legislation, resulting in the Kyiv princedom's first set of laws, "Ruska Pravda" ("The Truth of Rus"). This body of law held considerable influence over all later laws up to the times of the hetmanate. Over the course of Yaroslav's rule in Kyivan Rus, about 400 churches were built.

The most well known monument to Yaroslav the Wise is located near ***the Golden Gates in Kyiv***. Based on a design by the sculptor Ivan Kavaleridze, the bronze figure of the Prince holding the miniature of St. Sophia Cathedral is jokingly called "a man with a cake" by Kyivans

The Order of Prince Yaroslav the Wise is the title of the State Award for distinguished service to Ukraine

The most prominent of these is St. Sophia Cathedral. The Cathedral is the most prominent architectural monument of the princedom times. It is a UNESCO World Heritage site and an important symbol of Ukraine's endurance. Inside, a fragment of a wall painting has survived depicting the prince's family — including his daughters, whom Yaroslav later married off to European royalty, thus strengthening Kyivan Rus's ties to Europe. Yelisaveta became the queen of Norway, Anastasiabecame the queen of Hungary, and Anna became the wife of Henry I and the queen of France. Quite the legacy!

Each of the prince's daughters received a dowry: books from Yaroslav's library. This legendary collection of books and documents, which was kept in St. Sophia Cathedral, became the first library of Kyivan Rus. In addition to numerous religious texts, the library also contained translated works on geography, astronomy, philosophy and history. Enthusiasts are still trying to track down Yaroslav's collection.

4

Anna Yaroslavna

Highly educated, multi-lingual and politically astute, Anna was the sixth Queen of France

Anna Yaroslavna (born c. 1024) was the daughter of Yaroslav the Wise, the grand prince of Kyiv. He is sometimes known as the "father-in-law of Europe" because of how he established blood relations by marrying his daughters to the most influential European monarchs of the time. Like her siblings, Anna Yaroslavna also bore this fate. She married the French King Henry I, becoming the sixth queen of France. The French nicknamed her Anne of Kyiv.

Anna Yaroslavna left ***graffiti on the wall of St. Sophia Cathedral in Kyiv*** in the eleventh century. It is preserved to this day

Anna was educated, cultured, and known for her diplomacy in the conduct of affairs of state. Because of this, she had a hand in governing and her mark can be found on official documents from the time.

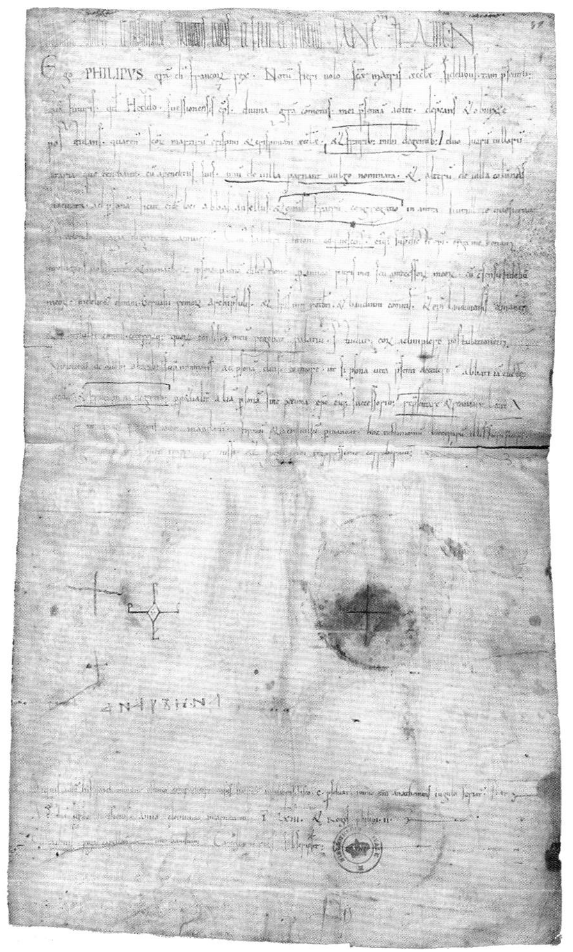

A charter signed by Anna, 1063

During Vladimir Putin's visit to France in May 2017, the president dated the French-Russian friendship back to the eleventh century, when Anna, whom the president called "Russian Ani," became the queen of France

Ukraine's official Twitter immidiately posted a response, pointing out that ***Moscow didn't even exist at that time, so it doesn't make sense to call Anna Russian***

After the death of Henry I, Anna left the court for several years. She reappeared on the political horizon in France when her son Philip became king. Anna Yaroslavna's fate after 1075 is unknown, yet this woman has forever entered the history of France not only as an impressive persona, but also as the great-grandmother of many French kings.

As the wife of Henry I, and as Regent for her son, Philip I, ***Anna's signature in old Slavonic*** can be found on official state documents from the period

5

Magdeburg Rights

A medieval system of town privileges that guaranteed townspeople autonomy from the state and from greedy feudal lords

In the fourteenth and fifteenth centuries Kyiv became part of the Polish-Lithuanian Commonwealth. Prince Alexander Jagiellon I granted the city the Magdeburg rights, to allow the Kyivan guilds and trade to flourish, to encourage support for the Commonwealth among its citizens, and to reduce the power of the big feudal lords. Over the next few years the Kyiv Magistrate was formed, a new governing body which was based on what is now Kontraktova Square.

The Magdeburg Law protected the guilds and local artisans and ensured the election of two magistrate colleges — the Lava, headed by a ward, as well as a council which had the burgomaster (or mayor) as its head. The former functioned as a criminal court, and the latter attended to administrative issues. The members of the magistrate were chosen by wealthy townspeople, whereas the burgomaster was chosen by the councillors.

When Kyiv was granted the Magdeburg Law, the city authorities could now develop the city more freely, own land, and collect taxes, as well as trade. For the first time, any taxes collected could go into developing the city, rather than going straight into state coffers. During this period Kyiv saw a real economic boom, and its citizens had civil rights and freedoms. The Magdeburg Law was officially repealed in 1834 under Nikolai I's reign.

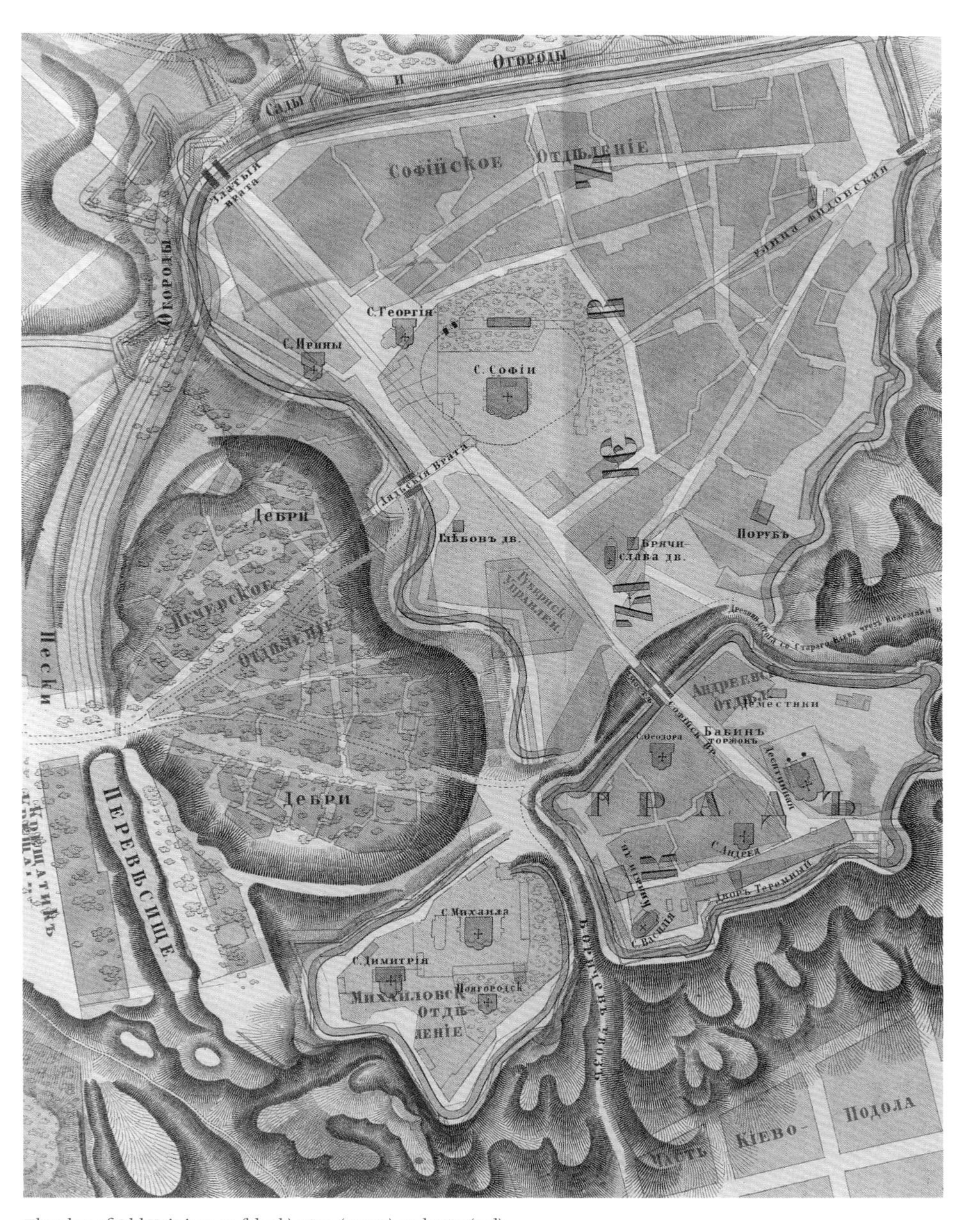

The plan of Old Kyiv in 1240 (black), 1800 (green) and 1964 (red)

6

Ivan Mazepa

The most renowned of all the hetmans of Ukraine — he is featured in 17 works of literature, 186 engravings and 42 paintings

Hetman Ivan Mazepa has inspired artists from Byron and Hugo to Vernet and Liszt. His renown and intrigue stems in part from a reputed incident at the Polish king's court. According to one tale, Ivan had an affair with the wife of an influential Polish magnate. Mazepa eventually returned to Ukraine, entered into the service of hetman Petro Doroshenko, and participated in several military campaigns. Later he served under Doroshenko's rival as well, Ivan Samoilovych, where he quickly gained the man's confidence and rose through the ranks.

It wasn't until Ivan Mazepa was almost 50 years old that he was elected hetman and received the hetman's mace (*bulava*). Mazepa's rule lasted 22 years. During this time, Ukraine was on the rise — industry, trade, and culture flourished. The hetman supported Ukraine's educational literary and cultural development. Through his patronage,

The Church of All Saints in Kyiv Pechersk Lavra was built through Mazepa's patronage. It is a prominent example of Cossack (Mazepa style) baroque

The popularity of Byron's poem about the hetman has led to several towns in the United States and the National Park in Queensland, Australia, ***being named after Mazepa***

Top: Horace Vernet, ***Mazepa Pursued by Wolves****, 1833*
Left page: Unknown author, ***Portrait of Ivan Mazepa***

numerous works of Ukrainian literature were printed, and a vast number of buildings and churches were constructed and restored. This architectural legacy has its own unique style: "Mazepa baroque."

Mazepa's epoch came to an end with the Northern War. Tsar Peter I of Russia's persistent attempts to annihilate Ukraine led hetman Mazepa to seek an alliance with King Stanislaus I Leszczyński of Poland and King Charles XII of Sweden. When this alliance was defeated, Mazepa was forced to leave the country forever. To subjugate Ukrainians, the tsar ordered the hetman's capital, Baturyn, to be ruined. He also ordered the Russian and Ukrainian churches to anathematize Mazepa. Mazepa died in exile in Moldova. Despite the efforts of Russian and Soviet propagandists to paint Mazepa as a traitor, Ukrainians know better — Mazepa is a symbol of Ukraine's long and ongoing fight for independence.

7

Kyiv Governorate

In 1710, Kyiv was subsumed into the Muscovite kingdom as the center of the Kyiv Governorate

When Kyiv became part of the Russian Empire, local self-governing bodies which were under the Magdeburg Law were gradually squeezed out, and Kyivites became effectively removed from any say in their government. This newly-created administrative entity was headed by the governor-general, who was appointed by the Russian tsar.

Due to the development of industry and capitalism, Kyiv became a center of trade and the economic life of the whole Russian Empire. As a result, the city began to expand, and merchants, gentry, the military classes, and free-men began settling in greater numbers in Kyiv.

At the beginning of the nineteenth century, the city was divided into five main districts: the Pechersk quarter, Old Kyiv, the Palace Quarter, Podil, and the Ploska settlement. The next few decades saw the addition of the Lybidska quarter, Priorka, Kurenivka, Syrets, Shuliavka, and Zvirynets. Some of these administrative units have preserved their names to this day.

A huge fire in Podil in 1811 destroyed practically the whole neighborhood. Its redevelopment plan meant that its streets were to be laid out in a grid around Kontraktova Square, whereas before they were built radiating out in

The Kyiv Governorate was ***one of the first eight governorates*** created under Peter the Great's reforms

It was dismantled finally in 1925, with the transition to a Soviet system of government (with areas divided into center-okrug-region)

Top: The map of the Kyiv Governorate in 1812
Left page: The emblem of the Kyiv Governorate

a circular fashion. New and expensive materials were used for the renovation, such as stone, iron, brick, and alabaster.

Kyiv saw its first construction boom with new mansions for the aristocracy, and government buildings being built. For the first time, housing had to be commercialized, and so Kyiv's first hotels, barracks, workers' houses, and "profitable buildings" sprang up, where the city's new settlers could find a place to rent.

Toward the end of the nineteenth century, voting rights for Kyivites were based on property ownership — in particular, owning big capital, which meant that local government depended on bankers, factory owners, merchants, and big landowners. Kyiv's administrative center was then moved to Khreshchatyk.

8

Mykhailo Hrushevskyi

Held by many to be Ukraine's first president — in 1917–1918 he was the head of the Central Rada of the Ukrainian People's Republic

Mykhailo Hrushevskyi was a Ukrainian intellectual, patriot, revolutionary and politician. He faced persecution by authorities throughout his life for his dedication to Ukrainian independence.

Hrushevskyi was born in 1866 to the family of a teacher; he grew up smart and inquisitive. He was fond of Ukrainian literature and wrote his first literary works during his school years. While a student of history at St. Volodymyr University, he was politically active and arranged secret meetings of a Ukrainian group in his home. The tsar's government persecuted Hrushevskyi for such activities, but he remained stalwart and actively participated in the 1917 revolution for Ukrainian independence. As empires crumbled and reformed, a new wave of optimism arose in Ukraine. In 1917, the Ukrainian Central Rada was founded in Kyiv, and Hrushevskyi was unanimously elected its chairman. Following the success of the Bolshevik revolution in Russia, hopes for autonomy inside Russia were lost, and Mykhailo Hrushevskyi declared the independence of the Ukrainian People's

The 10-volume ***History of Ukraine-Rus'*** is the life's work of Mykhailo Hrushevskyii. This series gives the most comprehensive overview of the history of the Ukrainian people from ancient times to the late seventeenth century

Republic. Independent Ukraine adopted the blue-and-yellow flag and the trident as its national emblems. Its anthem, "Shche ne vmerla Ukraina," (Ukraine is not yet dead) was a poem by Pavlo Chubynskyi set to music by Mykhailo Verbytskyi. All these remain official symbols of the State to this day.

The optimism of 1917 was short-lived. In April 1918, hetman Pavlo Skoropadskyi led a coup against the Hrushevskyi government with the support of the German army. An authoritarian right-wing government was installed and Hrushevskyi was forced to leave the country. Later, he returned to Soviet Kyiv, where he continued his scientific work and became the head of the All-Ukrainian Academy of Sciences. But his life was not easy as the Soviet government persecuted him until his death in 1934. Mykhailo Hrushevskyi was a prolific researcher; the complete collection of his works comprises 50 volumes of historical, social and political works, fiction and literary criticism.

9

Babyn Yar

A ravine tucked away in one of Kyiv's residential neighborhoods is the site of unfathomable horror — between 100,000 and 150,000 Roma, Jews, Ukrainians, and many others were murdered here by the Nazis during the Second World War

Today, Babyn Yar is a lush park in a quiet residential area of northwestern Kyiv. In Soviet times, there were plans to build a ski facility here. But the German occupation changed these plans and forever changed the ravine. Instead, it became the site of one of the greatest massacres carried out by the Nazis during the Second World War.

At the end of September 1941, Nazi invaders occupied Kyiv, and under the threat of the death penalty, ordered all Jews in the city to gather near Babyn Yar. En mass, Kyiv's Jewish residents were ordered to undress, all their valuables were taken from them, and then, in groups, they were lined up and shot. Body after body — men, women, children — piled up in the ravine. In just two days, thirty-four thousand people were executed here. These mass executions were repeated again and again over a span of two years. The victims included Jews, Roma, prisoners of war, members of the resistance, and Soviet and Ukrainian intellectuals. In their retreat from Kyiv, the Nazis tried to hide the evidence of their crimes. But historians have managed to estimate the number of victims — somewhere between 100,000 to 150,000 people were murdered at Babyn Yar.

This horrifying massacre has been documented by Anatoly Kuznetsov in *Babi Yar: A Document in the Form of a Novel*. Kuznetsov smuggled his novel of the horrors of Babyn Yar out of Soviet Russia, and it was eventually published in the United States in 1970. The Soviets tried to hide the Jewish nature of the massacre at Babyn Yar. It was only under an independent Ukraine that memorials commemorating the fate of Jewish victims were finally erected. Kuznetsov's book ends with a chilling warning: "I have not recounted anything exceptional, but only about ordinary things that were part of a system; things that happened just yesterday, historically speaking, when people were exactly as they are today."

Twenty years later, Babyn Yar became the location of another tragedy. In 1961 the dam that crossed the ravine collapsed. Torrents of dirt and water broke loose on the city streets, sweeping everything away in the process — buildings, vehicles, people. This tragedy is sometimes referred to as "Kyiv's day of Pompeii" — over 1,500 people died.

Olena Teliha Street — located in front of Babyn Yar — is named after a well-known Ukrainian poetess who was executed in the ravine along with other nationalist writers in February of 1942

There are numerous memorials to Babyn Yar throughout Kyiv. At the site of the massacres you will find the 1976 monument to Soviet citizens and prisoners of war shot at Babyn Yar, and nearby, the 1991 monument to Jewish victims. There are many more throughout the city, and even internationally — in Israel, Australia, and the United States

10

Independence Day

Independence Day is celebrated on August 24 to commemorate Ukraine's 1991 Declaration of Independence

The Act of the Declaration of Independence of Ukraine was adopted by Ukrainian Parliament on August 24, 1991, establishing Ukraine as an independent state. On this day, Parliament called for an independence referendum to support the declaration. The resulting referendum on December 1, 1991 was unequivocal — more than 90 percent of Ukrainians voted in favor of independence with a high voter turnout of 82 percent.

Today, Ukraine's independence takes on new meaning. Its centuries-long fight for independence continues with Russia's invasion of eastern Ukraine and its ***annexation of Crimea***

Ukraine had sought independence from the Soviet Union for decades, and by the late 1980s, calls for democratic reform were overpowering. Several movements buoyed these aims. The Ukrainian miners' strikes between 1989 and 1990, and the Granite Revolution (also known

АКТ
ПРОГОЛОШЕННЯ
НЕЗАЛЕЖНОСТІ УКРАЇНИ

24 серпня 1991 р.

Виходячи із смертельної небезпеки, яка нависла була над Україною в зв'язку з державним переворотом в СРСР 19 серпня 1991 року,

— продовжуючи тисячолітню традицію державотворення в Україні;

— виходячи з права на самовизначення, передбаченого Статутом ООН та іншими міжнародно-правовими документами;

— здійснюючи Декларацію про державний суверенітет України, Верховна Рада Української Радянської Соціалістичної Республіки урочисто проголошує незалежність України та створення самостійної української держави – України.

Територія України є неподільною і недоторканною.

Віднині на території України мають чинність виключно Конституція і закони України.

Цей акт набирає чинності з моменту його схвалення.

Верховна Рада України

Top right: ***The Act of the Declaration of Independence of Ukraine****, established Ukraine as an independent state*

as the Student Revolution) in 1990 supported the cause of independence.

Independence Day is Ukraine's most popular holiday, and Kyiv is a great place to take it all in. Put on a *vyshyvanka* (traditional embroidered shirt), drape yourself in blue and yellow, and head to Khreshchatyk for open-air concerts, parades, and other festivities!

Leonid Kravchuk served as independent ***Ukraine's first president***, from December 5, 1991, until his resignation on July 19, 1994

11

Orange Revolution

A series of protests and political unrest that took place in Ukraine from late November 2004 to January 2005

Ukraine's 2004 presidential election was marred by massive corruption, voter intimidation, and electoral fraud. This sparked a massive peaceful protest movement against the ostensible president Viktor Yanukovych and his party. Kyiv became the focal point of the movement's campaign of civil resistance, with thousands of protesters demonstrating daily.

Nationwide, the democratic revolution was supported by a series of acts of civil disobedience, sit-ins, and general strikes. It was organized by the failed presidential candidate Viktor Yuschenko and his party and supporters. The color orange was adopted to unite all those who fought against the corrupt elections, along with the word "Tak!" ("Yes!"). The nationwide protests succeeded when the results of the original count were annulled, and a revote was ordered, resulting in Yushchenko's victory.

"Razom nas bahato! Nas ne podolaty!" This chant spread through the crowd of hundreds of thousands that filled Kyiv's Independence Square during the Orange Revolution

"Together, we are many! We cannot be defeated!" emerged from a sea of orange, signaling the rise of a new democratic Ukraine

Viktor Yanukovych holds the special status of sparking not just one, but two revolutions

The first, due to election fraud in 2004, and the second during the 2013–2014 Euromaidan Revolution when ***he ordered protestors to be beaten and killed***

12

Euromaidan

Ukraine's Revolution of Dignity — a political, social and cultural transformation

Kyiv's Maidan Nezalezhnosti (Independence Square) is the city's central square — a meeting place to stroll, flirt, people-watch, and debate. It has long been the focal point for numerous protests and is, quite simply, the center of Ukraine's political consciousness. It was the site of mass protests against president Kuchma in 2001 and the Orange Revolution in 2004.

Euromaidan gave way to many cultural initiatives, among them ***Artists Support Ukraine***, aimed at turning international attention toward the current situation in Ukraine

At the end of November 2013, president Yanukovych reneged on a promised trade agreement with the European Union, sparking a peaceful protest movement against this hasty reversal. A subsequent violent crackdown on peaceful protestors (along with the passing of draconian anti-protest legislation) cemented broadscale support for political change. The scope of the protests evolved over the coming weeks, and millions of Ukrainians came out on the streets to demand a democratic government. Widespread grievances of government corruption, abuse of power,

violation of human rights, and profound economic mismanagement led to calls for president Yanukovych's resignation. Through the cold winter months, "Maidaners," as they came to be called, set up camps, barricades, kitchens, medical services, an open university, and even a library to support the cause.

Events came to a head at the end of January when several protestors were killed. In the following month, more blood was spilled — the regime's brutal Berkut (Eagle) special forces and government snipers killed dozens of men and women and wounded thousands.

At the end of February, president Yanukovych gave an ultimatum to the protest movement — "pack up and leave the Maidan." But the Maidaners remained, stalwart: they weren't going anywhere. The deadline to leave came and went. Yanukovych fled to Russia, and a provisional government was formed.

Serhiy Nigoyan was an Armenian-Ukrainian activist. He was the first protestor killed by shooting during the Hrushevskoho riots in January

CULTURE

*Right page: Oleksandr Murashko, **Parisian cafe**, 1903, the Kharkiv Art Museum*

13

Vladyslav Horodetskyi

A creative, whimsical, and imaginative architect, entrepreneur, and philanthropist

Vladyslav Horodetskyi (1863–1930) is of Polish descent, but he made Kyiv his home for thirty years and left an incredible architectural mark on the city. Horodetskyi designed buildings and entire streets. His most famous creations are the National Art Museum, the House with Chimaeras, and the St. Nicholas Roman Catholic Cathedral, all built in pseudo-gothic style. Many consider the House with Chimaeras the most unique building in Kyiv. This architectural and sculptural masterpiece is built on a steep slope, and its facade is ornamented with dozens of concrete animals and mythological creatures. Besides his work in Kyiv, Horodetskyi has also designed buildings in Cherkasy, Uman, and other Ukrainian cities.

Thanks to the renowned architect's devotion to Art Nouveau, he was nicknamed "Kyiv's Gaudi." One of the main streets in Kyiv is named in his honor.

After the arrival of Soviet authorities, the architect emigrated first to Poland and then to Teheran where he designed several remarkable buildings, including the Shah's palace.

House with Chimaeras
10 Bankova Street, Kyiv

14

Kazimir Malevich

An avant-garde artist and theoretician of Ukrainian-Polish descent

Malevich's works are held in several major art museums, including the State Tretyakov Gallery in Moscow, the Museum of Modern Art and the Guggenheim Museum in New York

Kazimir Malevich the leader of the avant-garde suprematist movement. Malevich was born in Kyiv and spent his childhood moving around Ukraine with his family. At the age of sixteen, he began studying at the Mykola Murashko Kyiv Drawing School. In 1904, Malevich moved to Moscow and participated in several exhibitions. In 1915, Kazimir Malevich started a new trend in art: suprematism. His most iconic work in this style is the renowned *Black Square* painting.

From 1919 to 1930, Malevich was busy teaching and writing. He taught at the Vitebsk Practical Art School in the USSR, which

*Kazimir Malevich, **Black Square**, 1915, the State Tretyakov Gallery, Moscow, Russia*

was headed by Marc Chagall at the time. He was also one of the founders of the State Institute of Artistic Culture in Leningrad, and taught at the Kyiv Art Institute. Malevich passed away in Leningrad in 1935, leaving behind not only outstanding works of art, but also a considerable body of literature.

Suprematist Composition by Malevich was sold at a Sotheby's auction for more than ***$60 million*** in 2008

15

The Bohdan and Varvara Khanenko Museum of Arts

The story of the love between two art connoisseurs who gave Ukraine its greatest collection of art

She was the daughter of a Ukrainian sugar trader and philanthropist, and he was the descendant of a hetman leader from the Right Bank of Ukraine. Varvara Tereshchenko and Bohdan Khanenko married in 1874, honeymooning in Europe, where they brought back their first paintings. Their collection started here, growing over the years with countless pieces of art.

At the beginning of the twentieth century, in their estate on Tereshchenko Street, the couple opened a museum which exhibited pieces of ancient European and Oriental art. Bohdan's death, followed by Varvara's, as well as the turbulent historical events that were to follow, determined the fate of the museum and its directors. The Soviet authorities sold numerous treasures from the museum, and the occupying Nazis carted off hundreds of paintings and over 20,000 engravings. It was only thanks to the evacuation and the directors' decision to hide some of the work that they managed to save the collection, which now numbers around 25,000 pieces.

Since 2015, ***the People's Restoration project*** has allowed visitors to make donations to the museum toward the restoration of some of its display pieces. A 23,000-year-old Ancient Greek krater (a form of mixing vessel) was the first such piece restored under this project

The Khanenko museum also has ***a special focus on art therapy for people with disabilities.*** It offers tours for the blind and for the visually impaired, as well as sessions at the museum for people with learning disabilities

Clockwise: **The icon of Saints Sergius and Bacchus**; *Kunisada,* **Miya Station;**
Juan Bautista Martinez del Mazo, **Portrait of Infanta Margareta**
Left page: **Portraits of Bohdan and Varvara Khanenko**

Today, the museum has two permanent collections (European and Asian Art), and has themed temporary exhibitions. Among the collection's pieces are works by Pieter Brueghel the Younger, Peter Paul Rubens, Jacques-Louis David, and Francisco de Zurbarán, but the most famous painting in the collection is the portrait *The Infanta Margarita*.

16

Volodymyr Horovyts

It's hard to imagine a musical career more successful than that of Kyiv native Volodymyr Horovyts

Volodymyr Horovyts began his career as a composer and later worked as a pianist in order to feed his family during the difficult post-revolutionary years. Having emigrated to the West in 1925, Volodymyr Horovyts earned world fame as a musician. There were times when he would give 350 classical concerts a year. Audiences would even break their chairs in astonishment during his concerts in Paris. After his performance at Carnegie Hall, twenty-five-year-old Volodymyr Horovyts won the US over with his talent and virtuoso technique. In 1943, he raised a record-breaking sum of $11 million at a charity concert for the war effort.

In 1986, Horovyts was awarded ***the Medal of Freedom*** (the highest award that can be bestowed upon a US civilian). In that same year he returned to the USSR for the first time in sixty-one years for a series of sold-out performances

Horovyts was widely successful and accomplished. Since 1962, he has received twenty-four Grammy Awards, and in 1986, American president Ronald Reagan honored him with the presidential Medal of Freedom.

Kyiv Philharmonic

One of the Ukraine's most famous music institutions

The National Philharmonic was set up in 1863. However, nowhere had yet been found as a permanent venue for the institution, so famous musicians from all over Europe — among them Franz Liszt — came to perform at the contract fairs in Kyiv instead.

The building which today houses the Philharmonic was only built in 1882, but back then it was the Kyiv Merchants' Assembly, which held literary readings and concerts, family parties, masquerade balls, and charitable events, as well as mornings of chamber music. The prominent Ukrainian composer, Mykola Lysenko, also organized his music circles here, and the main concert hall is named after him.

In the 1930s, the Philharmonic was temporarily moved to the capital at the time, Kharkiv, but even after its relocation to Kyiv it still had not found a permanent residence. It was only in 1944 that the Philharmonic was finally relocated to the building which it resides in today. After the concert hall was restored and the

Among others, the composers ***Sergei Rachmaninoff and Alexander Scriabin***, and opera singer Feodor Chaliapin have performed there

During the Second World War ***the building was used as the German officers' mess***, and so it was preserved by the occupying forces

The prestigious library and archives of the Philharmonic were destroyed in a flood in the eighties

Bottom: Roman Kofman during conducting a musical performance

Symphony Orchestra was put together, the National Philharmonic of Ukraine finally began to look like the place that we know and love today.

Since 1972 the Kyiv Chamber Orchestra has been based there; one of its best-known artistic directors is Roman Kofman, an outstanding Ukrainian conductor, who was previously the general music director of the Bonn Opera.

18

Oleksandr Murashko

One of Ukraine's most internationally acclaimed painters — known for his vivid impressionism and compelling portraiture

Oleksandr Murashko — known for his colorful impressionist works of art — had a difficult upbringing. Born out of wedlock and unwanted by his mother, he lived with his grandmother in a small town in the Chernihiv Region until he was seven years old. He was then returned to the care of his mother, who had married the owner of an icon-painting workshop. This connection opened the world of art to the young Oleksandr. When the family moved to Kyiv, Oleksandr witnessed the painting of St. Volodymyr Cathedral. The work of the great masters — Vasnetsov, Nesterov, Pymonenko — made a deep impression on him, and he decided to dedicate his life to art. His stepfather, however, had a different plan for him: that Oleksandr continue icon painting for the family business.

Oleksandr Murashko received widespread international acclaim for his 1906 work "Carousel," which was awarded ***a golden medal at the Munich International Exhibition***. This recognition led to invitations to the top exhibitions across Europe

But Oleksandr could not be held back. He fled from home and wandered the streets of Kyiv, taking up any opportunity to

Left: Oleksandr Murashko, ***Parisian Cafe****, 1903, the Kharkiv Art Museum*
Right: Oleksandr Murashko, ***Winter****, 1905, the National Art Museum of Ukraine*

paint. Gathering his courage, he asked professor Adriyan Prakhov for help. Prakhov had noticed the boy's potential during his time in the Cathedral and together with Vasnetsov and Nesterov, helped Oleksandr get established in his chosen profession.

Murashko's talents were widely recognized. He studied at the St. Petersburg Academy and was a student in Ilya Repin's studio. He worked as a trainee artist in Paris and Munich, and his work was exhibited across Europe. Murashko settled back in Kyiv where his artwork continued to evolve. He is particularly known for his compelling portraiture. Today, you can find his work exhibited in some of the world's leading galleries.

Murashko was one of the founders of the Ukrainian Academy of Arts (the modern National Academy of Fine Art and Architecture). To enjoy Murashko's work, visit the National Art Museum of Ukraine ***www.namu.kyiv.ua***

19

Oleksandra Ekster

This highly accomplished and internationally respected painter and designer was a leader of the Ukrainian avant-garde movement

Oleksandra Ekster moved to Kyiv as a child from the town of Bialostok (now in Poland) where she was born in 1882. She graduated from the Kyiv Art School in 1906, married fellow artist Mykola Ekster, and settled at 27 Khmelnytskoho Street. Her studio in the attic became a meeting place for Kyiv's intellectual elite, including poets and writers, dancers and painters.

In search of inspiration, Ekster moved to Paris in 1908, where she became acquainted with many fascinating people, including poet Guillaume Apollinaire and artist Pablo Picasso. These new connections influenced her style — a peculiar combination of European culture and Ukrainian everyday life. Ekster experimented boldly with different styles, working in futurism, cubism, and avant-gardism. Her work and teaching led her to live in various cities, primarily Paris, Odesa, Kyiv and Moscow.

Oleksandra had many artistic talents — one of which was theater set design. Her theatrical scenery for *Romeo and Juliet* stunned audiences by unfolding across the entire space. She also designed the set

Photographs by the Author

JOKANAAN SALOME HEROD

COSTUME DESIGNS BY ALEXANDRA EXTER FOR THE CUBIST PRODUCTION OF OSCAR WILDE'S "SALOME" AT THE KAMERNY THEATRE, MOSCOW

Ekster created numerous illustrations to accompany the texts of ***Arthur Rimbaud, Omar Khayyam, Petrarch, Andre Gide, Horace, and Sappho.***

Ekster's paintings are regularly included in exhibits of constructivist and futurist art in major art galleries around the world, including ***the MoMA, the Thiessen, and the Tate***

She was an acquaintance of the Russian avant-garde painter ***Kazimir Malevich***, and a part of his artistic group Supremus

Top: Oleksandra Ekster, costume design for ***Romeo and Juliet****, 1921*
Bottom: Oleksandra Ekster, costume design for ***Salome****, 1917*

for Oscar Wilde's *Salome* in 1917, produced by Tayirov. The play was a triumph. Oleksandra was an innovator with successful exhibitions in Berlin, Paris, London, Prague, and New York.

The National Academy of Fine Arts and Architecture

The Academy has educated talented painters, sculptors and architects for almost century

The National Academy of Fine Arts and Architecture was founded in 1917 (known then as the Ukrainian Academy of Arts) by some of the country's most prominent creative intellectuals such as Oleksandr Murashko, Mykhailo Boichuk, Dmytro Antonovych and Hryhorii Pavlutskyi. Ukraine's revolutionary Parliament of the time — the Central Council under the leadership of Mykhailo Hrushevskyi — supported

One of the Academy foundrs was ***Oleksandr Bohomazov***, Ukrainian graphic artist and painter a member of the Ukrainian avant-garde movement

the creation of the Academy and it soon admitted its first students. During its early years it was a small school, teaching a limited number of academic disciplines, with few academic staff members and a small student body.

The Academy has gone through several changes over the last hundred years — shifting in scope and purpose and with name changes along the way. For a brief spell in the 1930s it was taken over as a center for Soviet cultural ideology.

Today, the National Academy of Fine Arts and Architecture provides education to over 1,000 students across the faculties of fine arts, architecture, and theory and history of arts. Over 160 professors teach within the Academy's 14 academic departments.

The Academy's gallery has regularly changing exhibits — with work from both up-and-coming and well-established artists. It's worth a visit: *www.naoma.edu.ua*

21

Serge Lifar

This Ukrainian held a tireless devotion to his motherland, despite having lived abroad for most of his life

Serge Lifar (1905–1986) was born in Kyiv and at the age of eighteen, emigrated to Paris to work in Sergei Diaghilev's Ballets Russes. In France he was destined to become a legend and a genius of twentieth-century ballet.

Lifar's memoirs, titled *Les Mémoires d'Icare*, were published posthumously in 1993

Lifar headed Paris's Grand Opera for more than three decades, staged more than two hundred performances, brought up a plethora of ballet stars, founded the Institute of Choreography in Paris, and occupied the honorable

position of the president of UNESCO International Dance Council. Serge frequently wore a *vyshyvanka* to his premieres, called himself a Cossack (his family had deep Cossack roots), and repeatedly refused French citizenship, offered to him by Charles de Gaulle.

From the time of his emigration, Lifar long hoped to return to Ukraine — his wish was fulfilled only in 1961 when he had a chance to visit his motherland.

In 1994, the Serge Lifar International Ballet Competition was founded in Kyiv. As one of the world's most significant ballet forums, these competitions have launched the careers of many rising ballet stars and choreographers.

You'll find an exposition dedicated to Lifar in the National Museum of History of Ukraine at ***2 Volodymyrska Street in Kyiv***

22

Opera House

Top architects from around the world competed to design Kyiv's Opera House

When you walk into Kyiv's famous Opera House, you're transported back in time to the early twentieth century. Its sumptuous interior with huge Venetian mirrors and a marble staircase matches its elaborate stage sets and embellished costumes.

The opera and ballet theater was constructed after a fire ruined Kyiv's main theater in 1896 — the first theater in Ukraine, where opera and drama troupes worked. An architect from St. Petersburg, Viktor Schroeter, won the contest for the best design. The main entrance to the magnificent neo-Renaissance building was meant to be decorated with the emblem of Kyiv, bearing the image of archangel Michael. But the Kyiv Metropolitan, who considered theater to be a sinful institution, ordered a change. Instead, winged women were placed there, who remain devoted patrons of the Opera to this day.

When the neo-Renaissance building was presented to Kyivans in 1901, it was roundly criticized for

The Assassination of Pyotr Stolypin*, Diana Nesypova*

Russian Prime Minister ***Peter Stolypin*** was assassinated at the Opera House in 1911. Some say you can sense his ghost wandering the corridors of the theater

The park near the Opera House Theater is a regular meeting spot for local skateboarders and alternative music fans

being ostentatious. But the theater has survived such complaints. It also survived being hit by an air bomb during the Second World War — which luckily didn't explode. In the 1980s, the theater's grounds were expanded and a park was added nearby. Today, the National Opera House of Ukraine can hold an audience of over 1,000 — quite often all of the seats are taken.

Between the theater seasons, the troupe successfully goes on tours in Europe, Japan, and the USA. When you visit, be sure to treat yourself to a caviar canapé and champagne, in the classic opera house tradition.

23

Icarus

This compelling mosaic on the wall of Kyiv's airport is a prime example of monumental painting from the 1960's

During the "Khrushchev Thaw era," Soviet artists took up new modes of self-expression while remaining within the boundaries of Socialist art. Mosaic monumental painting was among the most popular such art form — a hallmark of Soviet institutions from the 1960s. In Kyiv you'll find enormous proletariat-themed mosaic pictures on the walls of buildings along Victory Avenue or in the underground, such as the splitting of the atom, which you can find in Shuliavska Metro.

In Greek mytholog *Icarus was the son of the inventor Daedalus* who perished by flying too near the Sun with his wings made of wax

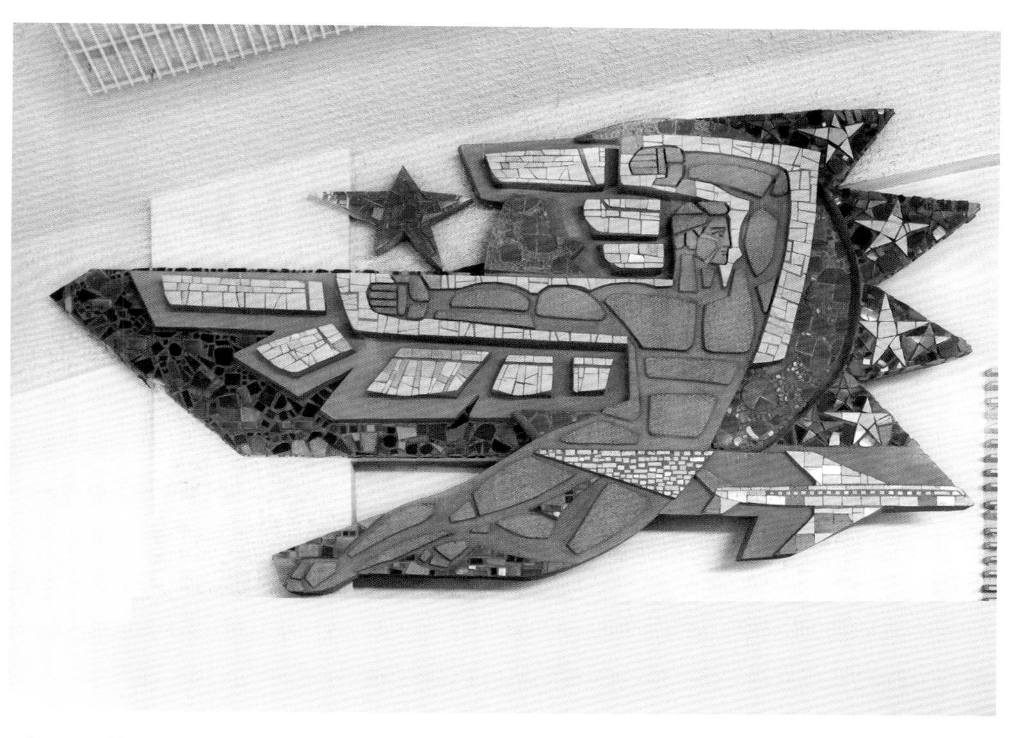

Valerii Lamakh, Ivan Lytovchenko, Ernest Kotkov, ***Icarus****, 1965, Terminal B of Boryspil International Airport, Kyiv region*

On the second floor of Boryspil Airport, you'll find a particularly brilliant example of monumental mosaic — *Icarus* by Valerii Lamakh. Lamakh was one of the brightest personalities of Kyiv's cultural life in the 1960s. As a teenager, he spent several years in Germany at a forced labor camp. After returning home, he entered the Institute of Arts — launching his career as a monumental artist. Lamakh's works are featured in Kyiv and many other cities throughout Ukraine. Despite the ideological constraints of the time, Lamakh's mosaics managed to express an individual vision. Over half a century later, his mosaics remain compelling works of art.

You may find more information about Soviet monumental mosaics in the book ***Decommunized: Ukrainian Soviet Mosaics***

24

Bulgakov House

The author of The Master and Margarita spent his childhood and adolescence in Kyiv

Despite the fact that Bulgakov's most famous novels were written when he no longer lived in Ukraine, his creativity is infused with Kyiv motifs. Bulgakov was born in 1891 at Vozdvyzhenska Street in Kyiv. His family subsequently moved many times, eventually renting an apartment on the Andriyivskyi Descent, where Mikhail spent more than a decade. This residence would later become the backdrop for the characters in his novel *The White Guard*.

Bulgakov showed a literary promise early on in life. He started writing at the age of seven and long dreamt of becoming a writer. Despite this interest, he was trained as a doctor, graduating with honors from the Kyiv University Faculty of Medicine. During the turbulent revolutionary years, he worked as a physician and surgeon, eventually opening a private practice in Kyiv.

In 1919, Bulgakov was mobilized by the Ukrainian Army to serve in the North Caucuses where

The Bulgacov House is located at ***13A Andriivskyi Descent***

The Bulgakov Museum collection boasts over ***3,000 display pieces***, 500 of which were owned by Bulgakov. Replicas of lost items are painted in white, adding to the Museum's enigmatic atmosphere

It is thought that Margarita flew to ***Kyiv's Bald Mountain*** for the Witches' Sabbath in The Master and Margarita

he fell desperately ill with typhus. It was an event that forever changed his life. In recovery he vowed to follow his passion and pursue writing. Bulgakov moved to Moscow, took up a position as newspaper correspondent to make a living, and otherwise dedicated himself to his craft.

Throughout his life as a writer in the Soviet Union, Bulgakov had a trying time. At times, he was shunned and his work was censored, while at other times he was lauded, even gaining the personal protection of Stalin. Bulgakov repeatedly expressed a desire to return to Kyiv. The city's landscapes, inhabitants, and spectacular frescoes of Kyiv temples provided him with an inexhaustible well of inspiration.

Since 1989, the Bulgakov Family house operates as a museum. Its exhibits combine a history of Bulgakov's life along with installations drawn from his fictional works. The museum offers guided tours filled with mystery, surprise and special effects. The house is also a venue for book presentations, classical music concerts and theatrical performances.

25

The National Art Museum of Ukraine

They call the National Art Museum's patrons "lions" — they stand guard over the art, like the stone statues at the entrance to the building

The museum was officially opened on December 23, 1904. Its title wasn't changed until Ukraine gained its independence, when it became the country's National Art Museum.

The first works on show in the museum were donated by the Kyiv intelligentsia, in particular by Bohdan Khanenko, Vikentii Khvoika and the Tereshchenko philanthropic family. Today, the museum has a collection of around 40,000 pieces, covering Ukrainian art from the times of Kyivan Rus' right up to the present.

The exhibits are separated by historical period and genre, such as iconography, Ukrainian baroque art, art from the Modern period, and the Ukrainian avantgarde. Separate rooms are devoted to Taras Shevchenko's art. The museum also has a separate section of Boichukist art, which was a unique movement in early twentieth-century Ukrainian art.

The National Art Museum of Ukraine is located at ***6 Hrushevskogo Street***

The museum is housed in ***a neo-classical building designed by Wladyslaw Horodecki***, who completed the unfinished vision of its original architect, Petr Boitsov, giving it a new lease on life

Clockwise: Unknown author, ***Resurrection****, Galicia region, early sixteenth century; Fedir Krychevskyi,* ***Beatrice****, 1911; Oleksandr Bogomazov,* ***Sharpening the saws****, 1927*

26

Dovzhenko Film Studios

Around 1,000 films and thousands of TV shows have been shot at the Kyiv Film Studio

Cinema has been an inseparable part of the life of Kyivans since 1896 when the Lumière brothers' films first debuted in the Bergonie Theater (where the Lesya Ukrainka Theater of Russian Drama is presently located). Kyiv's love of film took off. Within a few years, Kyiv's first film lending service was launched — the first one ever in the Russian Empire. Not long after, the first private and state-owned motion picture studios emerged.

The studio's ***architect*, *Valeryan Rykov*,** also designed the "Zhovten" Cinema Theater — the oldest cinema in Kyiv

The state-owned Dovzhenko Film Studios are one of the largest and most enduring of these — they first opened their doors in 1927. Valeryan Rykov's bold vision for the studios won the competitive design contest. His studios were incredibly grand, and massive in scale: a complex with a total area of

around 40 hectares, grounded by an immense central pavilion. It was a highly productive space; ten or fifteen film crews could work there at the same time. The construction was finished in 1928, and during that same year, the cinema factory presented its first three films.

The studio's films have been widely recognized, receiving ***75 international awards, 65 Soviet awards,*** and one Academy Award

The Kyiv cinema factory became a center of contemporary cultural life. It was home to some of the best producers. The legendary Dziga Vertov filmed the first sound-film of the studio, *Symphony of Donbas*, in 1931, and Mykola Ekk produced the first color film, *Fair of Sorochyn*, in 1939. Serhiy Paradzhanov worked on his film *Shadows of Forgotten Ancestors* at the studio, now recognized as an international classic. It was also home to Oleksandr Dovzhenko's *Earth*, which was declared one of the top twelve films of all time at the 1958 World Exhibition in Brussels. After Oleksandr Dovzhenko's death, the studio was named after him.

Mystetskyi Arsenal

Mystetskyi Arsenal is Ukraine's largest government art institution

Kyiv's Mystetskyi Arsenal (Art Arsenal) gives new meaning to the term "art not war." It was built as a military arsenal in 1784, as a part of the Kyiv fortress. The arsenal housed arms and hosted workshops on weapon repair.

Mystetskyi Arsenal was built by order of Catherine the Great and is ***one of the first buildings in Kyiv built in the classical style***

In 2006, its function was transformed, from arms, to art. Ukraine decided to set up a major arts and cultural center and museum within the building — the largest exhibition space in Ukraine. You'll find exhibitions, concerts, film screenings, lectures, and seminars, as well as interactive projects for children and teenagers across its fifty thousand square meters of space.

Since 2011, Mystetskyi Arsenal has hosted the international book fair and festival Book Arsenal, whose participants include Ukrainian and foreign publishers.

Mystetskyi Arsenal is located at ***10-12 Lavrska Street***

Since 2010, ***the Art Arsenal's Small Gallery*** has held regular exhibitions of Ukrainian artists. It also serves as an art studio for children

In 2019 Kyiv's Book Arsenal Festival was named ***Literary Festival of the Year*** in London

28

PinchukArtCentre

Contemporary Ukrainian art is gaining momentum

Quite a number of Ukraine's contemporary artists have found international success — Oleksandr Hnylytskyi, Oleksandr Roytburd, Vasyl Tsaholov, Arsen Savadov, Illia Chichkan, Borys Mykhailov, Zhanna Kadyrova, and the R.E.P. group among them. The Ukrainian art scene is vibrant, with numerous galleries and centers for contemporary art. The Izolyatsia Foundation, M17 gallery, the Centre for Contemporary Art, and Art Arsenal are leading arts institutions in Ukraine. But the most significant international centre for contemporary art in Ukraine is the PinchukArtCentre (PAC). World-renowned Ukrainian billionaire, businessman, and philanthropist Viktor Pinchuk founded the Centre in 2006.

In 2007, Ukrainian billionaire Viktor Pinchuk became the co-owner of British artist Damien Hirst's legendary diamond skull For the Love of God that sold for ***$100 million***

Zhanna Kadyrova, ***Untitled,*** *2014, Fear and Hope group exhibition*

Since its early days, the PAC has held many large-scale events — among them the retrospectives of Damien Hirst, Vik Muniz, and Sir Paul McCartney.

In 2007 and 2009, the PinchukArtCentre officially represented Ukraine at the fifty-second and the fifty-third Biennale in Venice — to great acclaim.

The PAC has introduced national and international awards for young artists. To profile the work of up-and-coming artists they've created the Collection Platform: Circulation — a temporary exhibition of Ukrainian and international contemporary artists.

PinchukArtCentre address is ***1–3/2 Velyka Vasylkivska Street, Block A***

29

Viktor Marushchenko

This Kyiv and Berlin-based photographer is widely acclaimed — his work is featured in solo and group exhibits around the world

Viktor Marushchenko's family moved to Kyiv from Novosybirsk in 1951, when he was just five years old. Despite Viktor's long-held interest in photography, he didn't think that his hobby could actually become a career, until one of his photographs was published in *Culture and Life* in 1975. With this accomplishment under his belt, Viktor switched paths — he abandoned his career as an engineer and started a degree in journalism. At the same time, he persistently submitted his photographs to various editorial boards. His tenacity paid off, and he was offered a press photographer position at *Soviet Culture*.

In 2004, Viktor Marushchenko founded a School of Photography in Kyiv. You can visi its official website ***www.marush-chenko.com***

Working at the newspaper allowed Marushchenko to travel extensively and build his photography portfolio.

Left: Viktor Marushchenko, ***Sviatoslav Richter****, Kyiv Philharmonic, 1980*
Right: Viktor Marushchenko, ***Enlistment into the Little Octobrists****, Lenin Museum, Kyiv, 1987*

During a trip to Switzerland, the director of Lausanne's Musée de l'Élysée (Museum of Photography) saw Viktor's photos and suggested that he should participate in a festival of Eastern European photography in 1990. It was an auspicious meeting. The festival launched Marushchenko's career, and he started receiving invitations to exhibitions around the world.

From 2009 Marushchenko has published ***"5,6" a magazine about photography***

Atmospheric desolate Chornobyl landscapes, scenes from the life of the inhabitants of the Donbas, and urban storylines from the outskirts of Kyiv are some of the themes featured in his work. The way Marushchenko portrays Ukrainian reality is reserved, yet vivid. His contemplative shots make a strong impression.

Docudays UA

The only international human rights documentary film festival in Ukraine

In 2019 the festiv[al] was attended by ***more than 22,000 viewers and participant[s]***

The festival is non-political and non-commercial. It starts every March in Kyiv, and its program includes a range of different events in the spheres of culture and human rights, which take place until the end of the year.

The Docudays UA team is a dedicated group of film lovers, and its influence is noticeable everywhere. The festival selection is diverse and daring, the venues full at almost every screening, and there are guests from around the world.

The best films are shown throughout the year in various regions of Ukraine within the Traveling Docudays UA Festival. It develops critical thinking among young people through cinema clubs and discussions of films with human rights experts.

Docudays UA helps young Ukrainian documentary filmmakers to produce their films at the DOCU/PRO industry platform, and publishes an annual catalog of new Ukrainian films for international promotion.

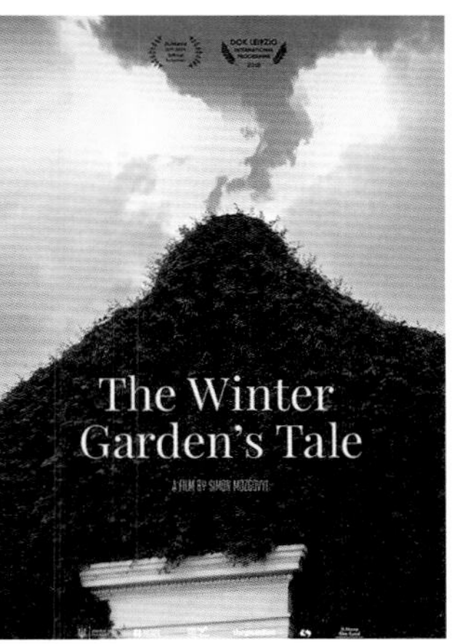

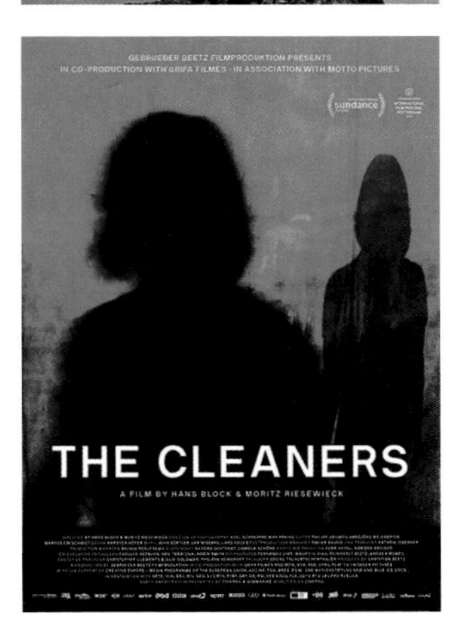

Clockwise: Maria Stoianova, ***Above the Styx****; Kim Hopkins,* ***Voices of the Sea****;*
Jon Kasbe , ***When Lambs Become Lions****; Simon Mozgovyi,* ***The Winter Garden's Tale****;*
Atsushi Kuwayama, ***A Friendship in Tow/Toe****; Hans Block, Moritz Riesewieck,* ***The Cleaners***

The festival's mission is to show the most talented and relevant documentaries from all over the world and raise the level of human rights protection in Ukraine. Docudays UA aims to facilitate the development of critical thinking, popularize and develop documentary filmmaking in Ukraine, and promote active citizenship and the treatment of human dignity as the highest value.

Check out
the festival website
www.docudays.ua

31

Closer

More than just a club — the bohemian Closer is Kyiv's creative center

Located on the grounds of an old ribbon factory in the historical district Podil, Closer is not only a night club, but also a café, showroom and record store that welcomes exhibitions and a summer veranda that opens out onto the picturesque Tatarka hills. As a nightlife venue, it is well-known for house and techno music raves that last from Friday night through to Sunday afternoon. Each party is planned in elaborate detail, from the artists' styles and the performance line-ups to the decor, which is unique from one weekend to the next.

Nearby Closer, at Nyzhnoyurkivska Street, there are other equally well-known clubs such as Mezzanine and Otel', the music space SHOOM and a radio station 20ft. Kyiv also has a few electronic music festivals up and running, such as Strichka or Brave! Factory, as well as famous nights like Rhythm Büro and CXEMA.

Kyiv techno-scene's rapid development, its underground nature and its role as a protest movement have made it an essential part of the city's cul-

ture. Some people aren't a fan of its label of "The New Berlin" — after all, Kyiv has its own character and obstacles that its citizens have to come up against, which make its rave culture a unique one. Young people just want to go out and have some fun, so why not do it whilst listening to a bit of techno?

FOOD

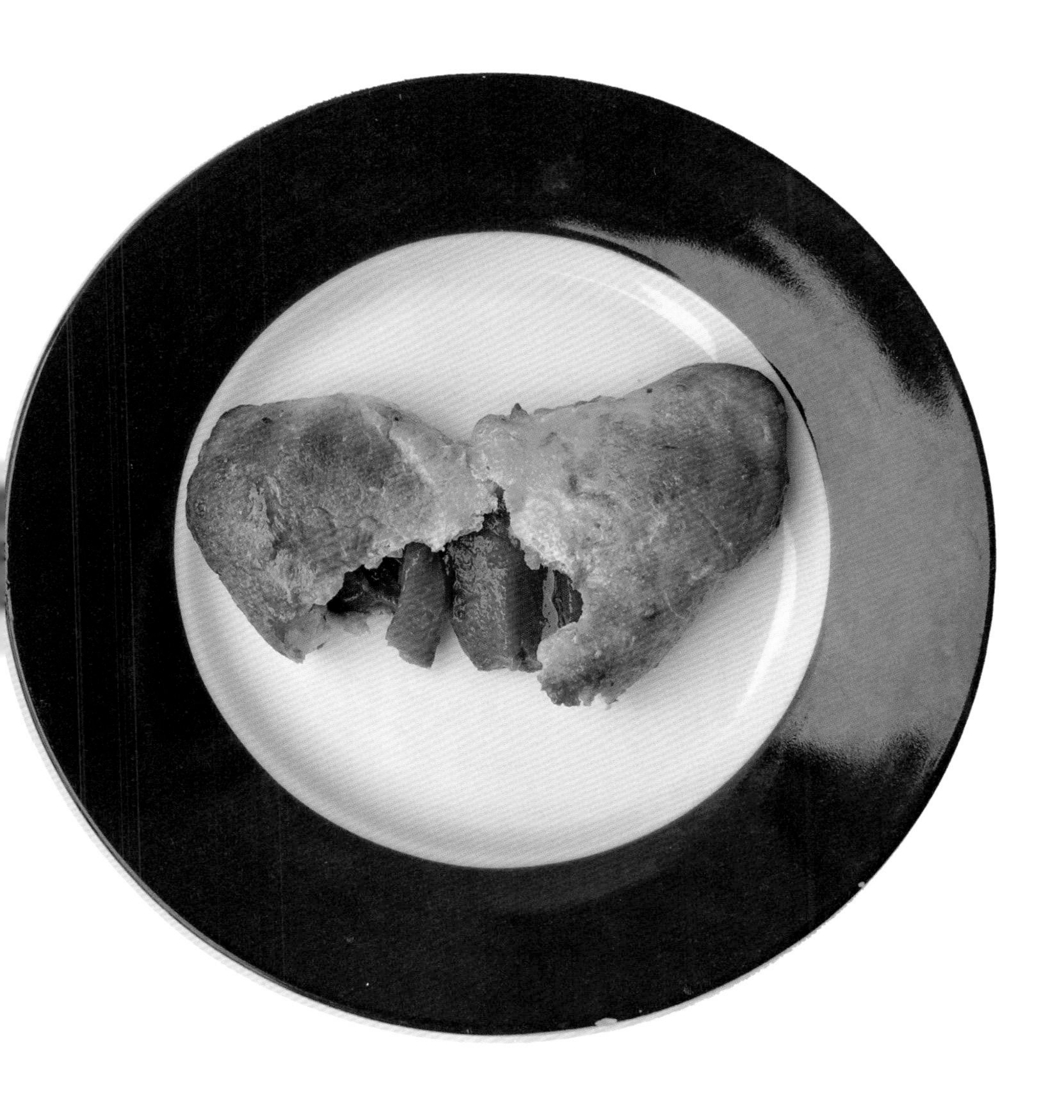

Chicken Kyiv

Pounded chicken breast, wrapped in butter and herbs, breaded and deep fried — simply divine

The ideal chicken Kyiv has a crisp fried shell with garlicky butter on the inside. Food lovers suggest two alternative modes of preparation. Old-fashioned recipes involve pounding the butter into the breast with a cooking hammer, giving the meat a tender creamy taste. Or you can wrap the butter (mixed with garlic and herbs) in the chicken. Cheese, mushrooms, and greens can also be added to the filling.

A classic chicken Kyiv is made with a chicken breast with the wing still attached

The origins of this dish are a matter of debate. Russians believe the dish was created in the 1970s for the opening of Kyiv's Moscow Hotel. A Ukrainian hotelier quoted in the *New York Times* dates the dish to 1819. The *Russian Tea Room Cookbook* credits Chicken Kyiv to the renowned French chef Careme at the Court of Alexander I. The food historian Vilyam Pokhlebkin also dates it to the tsarist regime.

Origins aside, this breaded, boneless chicken cutlet, cooked stuffed with butter and herbs, is a hugely popular dish. It's ubiquitous in its namesake capital... you'll find it on the menu at cheap fast food outlets and fancy restaurants alike. When you order the dish, just don't cut into it with your knife! Hot melted butter can squirt out and burn you, or at the very least make a big mess. Instead, pierce the dish with your fork, wait until the butter drips out, and enjoy.

33

Kyiv Perepichka

At the crossroads of Bohdan Khmelnytskyi and Khreshchatyk Streets, you'll always find a queue for Kyiv's legendary fast food

In Ukrainian national cuisine, *perepichka* is a delicacy of fried sour dough. Kyiv Perepichka takes this mouth-watering treat and adds a twist — the dough surrounds a sausage and is deep-fried. It's Kyiv's take on a sausage roll.

Kyiv Perepichka first opened in Soviet times, in 1981. The greasy, delicious snacks were sold out of a small kiosk in a prime location in front of the Central Universal Store at 3a Bohdana Khmelnytskogo Street. Kyivans took an immediate liking to the tasty, nourishing and cheap perepichka, which could be eaten on the go. The vendor's thin paper napkins — now, as ever — do little to keep your hands clean while eating this deep-fried delicacy.

Over the past 30 years, the center of Kyiv has changed a lot. There are so many new cafés, restaurants and fast-food outlets, and yet, people still flock to Kyiv Perepichka. If you're looking to try this great combination of national dish and classic hotdog, grab a spot in the line near Kyiv Perepichka's window. And don't worry — the line moves fast. The hard-working, experienced staff ensure that your wait is rarely longer than 10-15 minutes.

Kyiv Perepichka is open every day from 8.30 a.m. to 9 p.m. at *3a Bohdana Khmelnytskogo Street*

34

Salo

The French have foie gras, Ukrainians have salo — a traditional food made of salted pork fat

The importance of this popular Ukrainian food dates back to the Tatar-Mongol period. Over several centuries, Tatar-Mongols periodically attacked ancient Ukrainians, taking them prisoner and capturing their cattle. For religious reasons, the Muslim occupiers had no interest in consuming pork. Hence, it became a useful food for survival in hard times.

For preservation, salo is salted and sometimes also smoked and aged in a dark and cold place, where it will ***last for a year or more***

To visit Kyiv without trying authentic Ukrainian salo is tantamount to a crime! To find the best salo in the city, be sure to drop by the centrally located Bessarabska Market. Fur-

eft page: Salo in chocolate is a special Ukrainian treat

her afield, the Zhytnyi and Volodymyrsky markets also have a fine selection.

Picking out salo is a true art. It should be white, with a pinkish shade. The most tender pieces come from the back and the sides of a pig. Some people prefer "general's salo" — alo with more meat. At Kyiv markets you can find raw, alted or smoked, herbed, or spiced salo. You can eat it on its own; chop it and add it to *borscht* (beetroot soup) or on top of *arenyky* (dumplings); or have it sliced on rye bread, rubbed vith garlic, along with a shot of *horilka*. There are many ways o enjoy this tasty treat.

For a delicious salo tasting session check out the Bessarabka market at *2 Bessarabska Square*

35

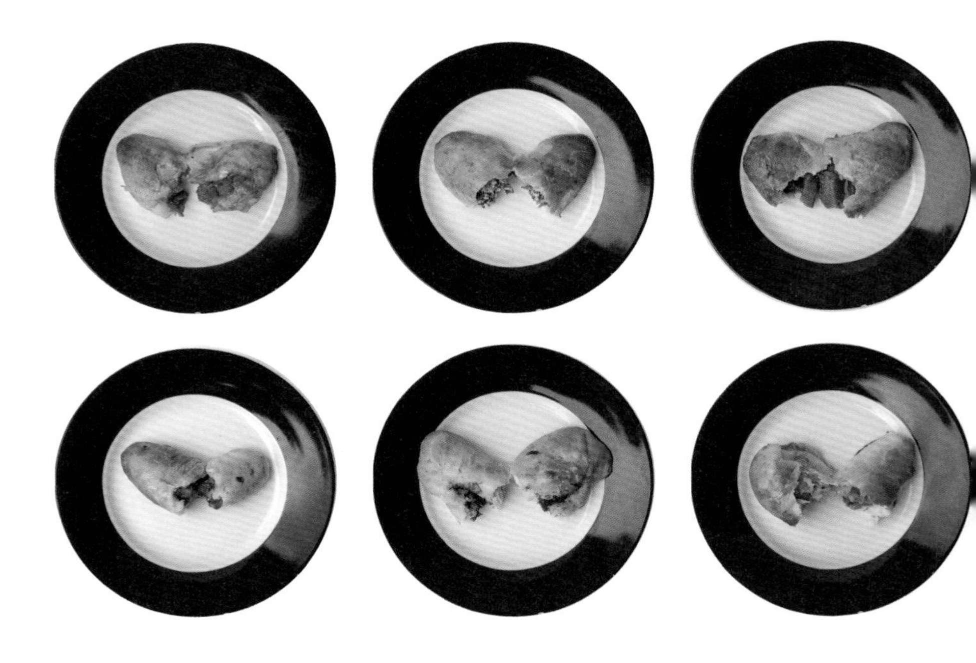

Yaroslava

The best buns in Kyiv!

Yaroslava is situated near the Golden Gates, in the very heart of Kyiv. On the first floor there's a big restaurant hall and a small shop with a bun take-away.

Yaroslava is one of the oldest restaurants in Kyiv. Yet, it is still very popular among the locals and visitors. There is always a line for the buns during lunchtime and in the evening. The buns have different fillings — sweet and salty — and are

Yaroslava is located at *13 Yaroslaviv Val Street*

ılways freshly baked. You should definitely try savoury ones
vith meat, with green onion and eggs, and with spinach, and
sweet buns filled with berries, and with cinnamon. Another
ip — order a hot bouillon to accompany the salty buns.

Downstairs there is a dining room, with a restaurant which
serves Eastern European food and is known for its borshch and
chicken Kyiv. It is a nice place to have a big dinner with friends
and to try all the tasty dishes the menu has to offer.

The cinnamon bun iis best to have with ***hot chocolate***

36

Kyiv Cake

This mouthwatering cake named after the capital can be found anywhere in Kyiv

Layers of crunchy meringue that melts in your mouth, surrounded by buttercream frosting and hazelnut chunks throughout — you won't find another cake like it! It's no wonder this is a favorite souvenir for visitors to bring back to their friends and family. You'll find pyramids of the white cake boxes with green chestnut leaves at Kyiv's Central Railway Station and Zhuliany or Boryspil International Airports — all ready for the trek home.

The recipe of Kyiv cake's layer and cream is ***a commercial secret***

In 2016, Kyiv cake celebrated its sixtieth anniversary. The recipe is said to have been invented thanks to a serendipitous mistake made by confectioners of the former Karl Marx Confectionary Factory (recently renamed Roshen). Today, the confectionary factory Roshen remains the leader in producing Kyiv cake — making around fifteen tons of the cake per night!

Київський торт®
ROSHEN
PREMIUM SWEETS
ROSHEN

37

Evening Kyiv Chocolates

Along with Kyiv Cake, visitors to the capital are sure to return home with a box of the city's most popular chocolates — Evening Kyiv

Kyivans love their sweet treats: pretty boxes of chocolates line every supermarket. Among them, Evening Kyiv chocolates are a favorite. Kyivans first tasted this delicacy — a whole nut covered in praline and glazed with chocolate — in 1984. It was an immediate hit, very different than the other plain Soviet sweets available at the time. The novelty of Evening Kyiv chocolates gave rise to a rumor that their manufacturing equipment was imported from behind the Iron Curtain, all the way from Switzerland or Germany.

Today, Evening Kyiv chocolates are produced at the largest confectionary in Kyiv, just like they were 30 years ago when they were first introduced. In Soviet times, the factory was named after Karl Marx. Today the factory produces over 100 types of sweets and is a part of the candy corporation Roshen, owned by Petro Poroshenko, former Ukraine's president.

While the popular chocolates with views of Kyiv on the box can be bought at any supermarket today, in Soviet times they were much harder

Over the past 30 years, ***the box's design has changed several times***, but the main image is always the same: a bright photo of the capital's center

o come by. You would have to wait endlessly in a shop's queue to buy them or else luck upon them, as a gift from well-connected acquaintances. The combined scarcity and popularity of the chocolates made them a cherished gift for friends and family — and also, an excellent bribe for bureaucrats needing a small nudge.

38

Mr. Pops

Even people who used to say they hate ice cream have become loyal fans of this ice cream startup

Founded in 2015, Mr. Pops began as a hobby for three like-minded friends, hoping to create a product that they would actually enjoy eating themselves. Soon, it grew into a successful startup in the local gastronomic scene and was first presented to a wide-scale audience at the Festival of Street Food. That's how a total popsicle obsession captured Kyiv.

The specialty of this product is the popsicle format, which was unknown to the Ukrainian consumer before, as well as all-natural ingredients and transparent packaging so the customer can see what they're choosing. Everyone who has tried this ice cream instantly appreciates the way the main ingredients are preserved for maximum flavor.

Great care has been taken to choose only the best ingredients. They source their mangos from India, passion fruit from the Dominican Republic, pistachios from Sicily

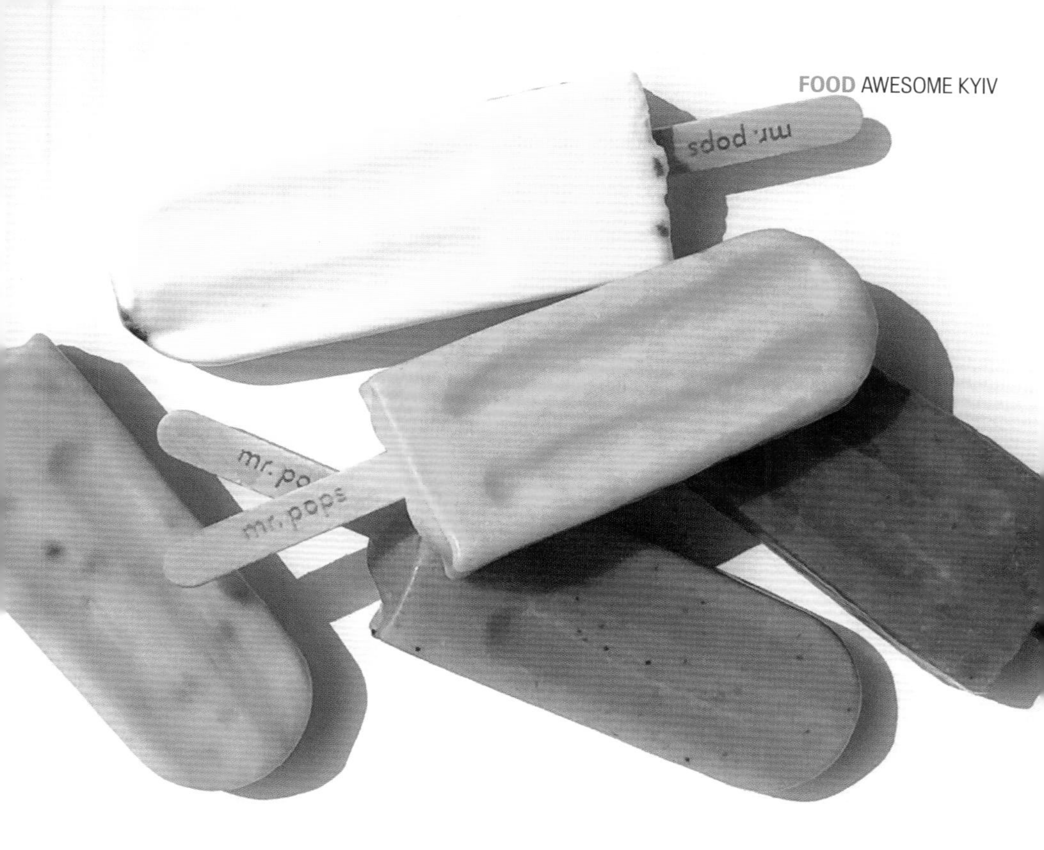

and Iceland, and strawberries from a local farm in Kherson.

Today, one can find an assortment of 15 flavors in Kyiv's grocery stores specializing in delicacies, craft food labels and wines, as well as in many cafes and coffee shops. The popsicles are also available for direct delivery.

Salted Caramel, Belgian Chocolate Eskimo, Toffee, Mango & Passionfruit, and Strawberry & Cream are just some of the flavors everyone loves. In addition, Mr. Pops offers unique flavors such as Pear with D'or blue cheese, Matcha and White Chocolate, and Vanilla with Brownie.

If you see people walking around the streets, looking very satisfied and taking photos of their popsicles, you can be sure they are from #mrpopsclub.

39

Adelle

This city-centre restaurant could fit right in on one of Tel Aviv's streets

Yevhen Gusovskiy together with well-known Israeli chef Alexey Krakovsky, developed the concept of a laid-back city café-restaurant with a tradition of Mediterranean food and Tel-Aviv vibes, where you can dine in comfort in a smart suit as well as in your pajamas.

Adelle is located in a two-story historical building at the two-story space with big glorious windows and old-fashioned molding on on the walls as a legacy from old times. The interior design is a perfect balance between homely restaurant and chic street food venue.

However, the reason for Adelle's popularity is obviously the food: not sophisticated, but simple, tasty and cooked with soul. In general, the food is less spicy than what's usually found in Israel, but some are very authentic, just like you would find in Tel-Aviv.

So, if you are into Israeli food and are looking for a place where sabih and hummus are as rich as rich as any you can find on Tel Aviv's Dizengoff Street and where burecas taste as good as at Carmel Market — Adelle welcomes you.

ISRAIR

40

Besarabka

For an authentic market experience, just head up Khreshchatyk toward Bessarabska Square

Merchants first occupied thissite back in the early nineteenth century. One could find goods from Southern Ukraine and present-day Moldova (Bessarabia) — hence the Market's present-day name. Bessarabka Market was one of the biggest in Kyiv. Back then it stretched all the way from Baseina Street to today's Sports Palace as a place of open-air trading.

In 1908, city authorities decided to house the Market under a roof. A competition for the best market building design was announced. The winning design came from Polish architect Henryk Gay. The Market's construction was sponsored by

Bessarabka translates to Bessarabia — a historical region that lays partly in current-day Moldova, which was occupied by the Red Army in the 1940s and subsequently integrated into the Soviet Union

When visiting, be sure to glance up at *the reliefs high up on the building's facade*. You'll see the "Milkmaid" and "Villager with oxen" — decorative panel pictures as well as geese on the metal gate

Kyiv residents consider Bessarabka *the most expensive Market in the city*. Hence the phrase "as expensive as at Bessarabka"

a local millionaire, sugar mill owner Lazar Brodskyi, who left the city 500,000 rubles to cover the roofed Market's construction costs.

The new Market opened in 1912. Having survived wars and revolutions, as well as several attempts to close it down (there were plans to build an art gallery in its place), it has somehow hardly changed to this day. You can still buy fresh fruit and vegetables, fish and meat, salo and dairy products, along with all kinds of gourmet food and fresh flowers. The Market also has a number of cafes, restaurants, and fast-food outlets selling shawarma and falafel.

PLACES

41 The Golden Gates **42** St. Sophia Cathedral **43** St. Kyrylo's Monastery **44** St. Volodymyr's Cathedral **45** Kyiv Pechersk Lavra **46** Podil **47** Kyiv-Mohyla Academy **48** Taras Shevchenko National University of Kyiv **49** Khreshchatyk **50** The Motherland Monument **51** Rusanivka **52** Crematorium **53** Tarilka **54** Borshchahivka **55** Picturesque Alley **56** Pyrohiv **57** Funicular **58** Salut Hotel **59** Friendship of Nations Arch **60** Metro **61** VDNG **62** Bursa **63** Circus **64** The Naked Room **65** Kyiv River Port **66** Kyiv Cycle Track

Right page: ***The Motherland Monument****, Kyiv*

41

The Golden Gates

In medieval times, Kyiv was a walled city with prominent Golden Gates announcing its main entrance

In the eleventh century, Kyiv was surrounded by an impregnable wall. A person could only enter the city through one of three grand gates. The Golden Gates, located to the south-west of the city, were a ceremonial entrance way, only opened for important guests such as visiting state ambassadors. There's a saying about the Golden Gates: you can only pass through them bearing good news.

In ancient times one could also enter Kyiv throug the Liadski Gates (now Independence Squareor "Maida Nezalezhnosti") and the Zhydivski Gates (now Lvivska square)

The Golden Gates were unbreachable. No conqueror was able to take them by storm: they even withstood the mighty Batu Khan. He and his forces held siege at the Golden Gates for a long time, but to little effect. Eventually, they stormed the city be breaching a part of the wall situated elsewhere.

As time passed, the Gates' defensive functions became obsolete. For many centuries, this once impressive monument was left abandoned and half-ruined. In the middle of the

eighteenth century they were covered with soil and disappeared from view entirely.

Today, you don't need use your imagination to visualize the Golden Gates — you can visit the site. The Gates you will see, though, are a reconstruction. Archeologists managed to find the remnants of the legendary city entrance and measured the exact dimensions of the Gates: their width was 10.5 meters, their height over 13, and their length almost 18. To protect the landmark, a museum was built over the ancient ruins; its design symbolically reflects the design of the historical structure.

Kyiv metro's Golden Gates station is located near the structure. It's decorated with inlaid panel pictures of Kyiv princes and ancient Rus temples. *The Daily Telegraph* named this station one of the best in Europe

Yaroslaviv Val Street is located where a defensive earthwork connected to the Golden Gates once stood

42

St. Sophia Cathedral

The oldest building in the city and the oldest Christian church on the lands of the East Slavs to have survived to the present day

Prince Yaroslav the Wise founded this cathedral at the beginning of the eleventh century. Since that time, Sophia Kyivska has survived dozens of Tatar-Mongol raids, multiple destructions and fires. Even nine centuries later, after numerous restorations and renovations, this cathedral was damaged once more, having been looted first by the Soviet authorities and then later by its Nazi occupiers. Today, the rebuilt cathedral is a designated UNESCO World Heritage site.

You can visit the Sophia Kyivska at ***24 Volodymyrsk Street***

*ꞏft page: **Mosaic of Oranta**, eleventh century*

The St. Sophia Cathedral contains breathtaking eleventh-entury mosaics. They embellish the altar and the central domes. he six-meter mosaic image of Oranta (Virgin Mary) is extraordi-ary. She appears to be in different poses depending on where you ook at her inside the cathedral. Be sure to check out the ancient rescoes from the eleventh to eighteenth centuries. The cathe-ral's grounds also house a necropolis — a burial place for promi-ent Ukrainian historical and religious leaders.

The St. Sophia Cathedral is without a doubt a unique master-iece of Ukrainian architecture. It's one of the main cultural and eligious centers of Orthodox Christianity and one of the most requently visited tourist attractions in Eastern Europe.

The Virgin Oranta (the Great Panagia) is a well-known Orthodox Christian depiction of the Virgin Mary in prayer with extended arms. ***The six-meter-high mosaic*** is located in the vault of the chancel. The icon is original to the cathedral — present since its foundation in the twelfth century

43

St. Kyrylo's Monastery

The only place you will find both ancient wall paintings dating from Kyivan Rus and monumental works of art from Mikhail Vrubel

St. Kyrylo's Monastery was founded in 1139 by the Prince of Chernihiv, Vsevolod Olheovych, to commemorate his victory in the struggle for Kyiv's throne. It is named after the Prince's patron saint — Kyrylo. At the time of its construction, the Monastery was located on the outskirts of Kyiv. Today it sits just around the corner from Spartak Stadium.

In almost 900 years of its history, Kyrylo's Monastery was pillaged by invaders more than once, stood abandoned for many years and was restored and renovated in different styles. Hetman Mazepa restored it using his personal funds. Later on, the Monastery was rebuilt under th supervision of the well-known architect, Ivan Hryhorovych-Barskyi, remade into a real masterpiece of th Ukrainian baroque style, but when the Russian Empress Catherine II visited, she did not like what she saw. She ordered its unique paintings to be whitewashed with lime, and turned it into a rest home for th mentally ill.

In the 1860s, students of Mykola Murashko Kyiv Art School

The sacred image ***"Holy Mother and Child"*** by painter Mikhail Vrubel was so widely esteemed that it launched his career. It is said that the Holy Mother's face is that of Adrian Prakhov's wife, with whom the painter was in love with at the time

Many generations of adventurers have tried to find ***Mazepa's treasure***, which is allegedly hidden somewhere in the Kyrylo caves

p: Mikhail Vrubel, ***Holy Mother with a Baby****, 1885*

estored the paintings under the ıpervision of professor Adrin Prakhov. The young painter ıikhail Vrubel participated in ıis restoration. By some miracle, ıe church remained untouched uring Soviet times, although the nique bell tower of the Church of Annunciation was demolished and the asylum was reopened within the Monastery's walls. Today, the dispensary is divided from the Monastery with a concrete wall, and the complex has received the status of a State Reserve.

44

St. Volodymyr's Cathedral

The main temple of Ukraine's Orthodox Church of the Kyiv Patriarchate was built to honor St. Volodymyr, who brought Christianity to Rus

Like most grand cathedrals, St. Volodymyr's took many years to build. The project was first conceptualized in 1852 to honor the canonization of Prince Volodymyr. The construction was planned to finish in time for the 900-year anniversary of the conversion of Kyivan Rus. Municipal authorities allocated land near St. Volodymyr University, and architect Ivan Shtrom designed a striking Cathedral in neo-Byzantine style with 13 domes. But the design was exceedingly costly and due to lack of funds was altered several times. The final design incorporated 7 domes and an elongated cross-in-square plan. Construction took longer than envisioned, and the first service in the Cathedral finally took place in 1896.

Professor Adrian Prakhov, who taught at the University of Kyiv, is said to have supervised the Cathedral's wall painting. He brought considerable experience, having previously worked on the

Viktor Vasnetsov, ***Christ Pantocrator****, the painting on the ceiling of St.Kyrylo's monastery 1885-1896*

The front side of the Cathedral is decorated with mosaic inlay by ***Oleksander Frolov***, the founder of the Russian Empire's first workshop of mosaic art

It's said that when ***Viktor Vasnetsov*** was working under the church dome, he fell and was caught and saved by a hanging metal hook. The painter would go on to recall this as a miracle of God

wall paintings of St.Kyrylo's monastery. His vision was to recreate the feeling of grandeur of ancient Kyivan Rus temples. For this, he engaged the best painters of the day — Viktor Vasnetsov, Mikhail Nesterov, Mykola Pymonenko and Mykhailo Vrubel.

After the October Revolution, the Cathedral lost its bells when they were melted down for metal. Under Soviet rule the temple was spared destruction by leaders of the Communist party only because they decided to turn it into a museum of anti-religious propaganda.

45

Kyiv Pechersk Lavra

Lavra are large and important monasteries under direct authority of the highest church body

There are four lavras in Ukraine. The oldest and probably best known is the Dormition Kyiv Pechersk Lavra. This cave monastery was founded in 1051 during the rule of Prince Yaroslav the Wise, and it became the main center for Orthodox Christianity in Kyivan Rus. Kyiv Pechersk Lavra is currently a UNESCO World Heritage Site. The most outstanding landmarks of the monastery are the Great Lavra Belltower, the Monastery Caverns, the Dormition Cathedral, the Gate Church of the Trinity, and the Necropolis of the Kyiv Pechersk Lavra. The Lavra is also home to a number of museums and the National Historical Library of Ukraine.

Another main Orthodox center in Ukraine is the Holy Dormition Pochayiv Lavra in Pochayiv, Ternopil Oblast. According to legend, this monastery was founded by Kyiv Pechersk Lavra monks who

The Pechersk Lavra's secret underground tunnels have long intrigued all those who visit. They were built over a span of nine hundred years, starting in the eleventh century. You can walk through a small section today. At the moment, about 1,000 m² of the underground system has been explored

escaped the Tatar invasion of 1240. The main sanctuary of this lavra holds the miraculous holy icon of the Theotokos of Pochayiv, one of the most revered icons in the Orthodox Church.

Holy Dormition Sviatohirsk Lavra in Sviatohirsk, Donetsk Oblast, is Ukraine's third spiritual sanctuary. This monastery was built on the high right bank of Siverskyi Donets (on the so-called Holy Mountains). It includes a system of chalk caves, where monks still live to this day. According to some sources, this monastery has existed since the pre-Mongolian period.

The fourth Ukrainian lavra is the Greek Catholic monastery Univ Holy Dormition lavra of the Studite Rite. Among other things, this Lavra is famous for its Univ printing house, which was active between 1648 and 1770.

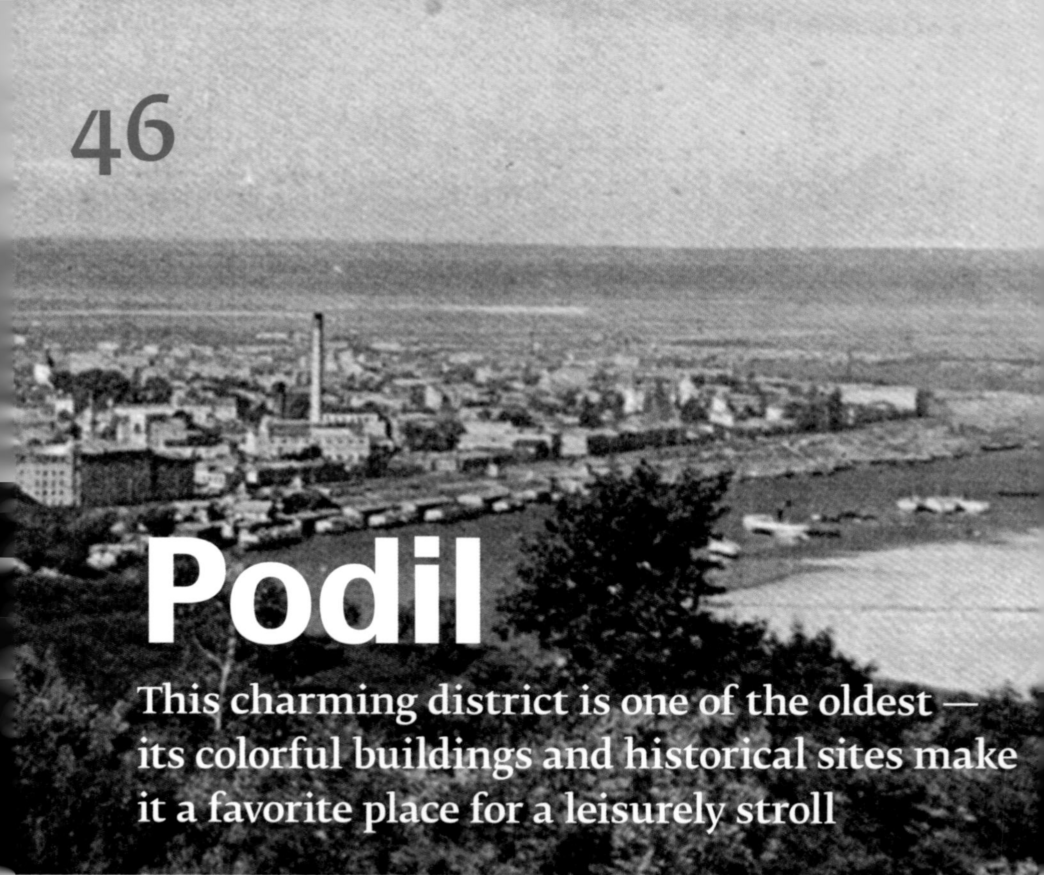

46

Podil

This charming district is one of the oldest — its colorful buildings and historical sites make it a favorite place for a leisurely stroll

Nestled in the lowland of the Dnipro's right bank, Podil has been inhabited as far back as the Stone Age. As you wander around the district, the reason becomes clear. Podil is an ideal location for trade, sitting on the river. At the time of Kyivan Rus it was home to artisans, and later, when the Tatar Mongol horde captured Kyiv and burned the Upper City, Podil became the main district of the capital. Ukraine's oldest university, Kyiv-Mohyla Academy, was founded in Podil.

A devastating fire in 1811 destroyed much of the historical district; more than half of the 3,672 buildings in densely populated Pod were obliterated. The city council resolved to rebuild the district in th then-modern classicist style. Many of those buildings have survived to this day — they are charming, colo ful and embellished.

At the heart of Podil you'll find :ontraktova Square. For centuries his was the center of business and rade life in Kyiv. Just as hundreds f years ago, you can wind your vay from the Upper City to Kon- raktova Square (the oldest square n the city) through the steep and vinding Andriyivskyi Descent, eferred to as "Kyiv's Montmartre." Iere, painters exhibit and sell their ictures, artisans sell utensils and souvenirs, and collectors sell unique vintage and antique curiosities. On the Descent you'll find St. Andrew's Church, the Mikhail Bulgakov Museum, and the famous One Street Museum, dedicated to the Descent.

This district's atmosphere combines old exquisite buildings, quiet streets, streetcars, churches and the famous Zhytniy Market. A walk around Podil is a truly unforgettable experience.

47

Kyiv Mohyla Academy

Ukraine's oldest university is one of the country's smallest, yet one of the best

Like so many Ukrainian institutions, Kyiv Mohyla Academy's history is a story of struggle for freedom and against foreign occupation. The University's legacy goes all the way back to the first educational institution in Kyivan Rus (and in Eastern Europe), which was founded by Yaroslav the Wise in 1037: Kyiv Academy, which had a good library, produced specialists in theology and other disciplines. After Rus was occupied by the Mongol Tartar horde, the Academy went underground, and lessons were given secretly, in monasteries and caves.

In 1615, this ancient educationa tradition was revived in part thanks to the patronage of noblewoman Halshka Hulevychivna, who gifted her estate to the Kyiv Brotherhood. The thankful brothers founded the Kyiv Brotherhood School, which merged with the Lavra School in 163 to form a Collegium. Metropolitan Petro Mohyla became the custodian of the collegium and turned it into a leading European educational institution where both clerical and secu-

eft page: Unknown author, ***Portrait of Petro Mohyla****, seventeenth century , the National Art Museum of Ukraine*

ıe University's motto reflects its long story: ***"Tempus fugit, Academia ·mpiterna"*** — "Time passes, but the ;ademy is eternal"

The Academy counts many famous people among its graduates — philosopher ***Hryhoriy Skovoroda*** and scientist ***Mykhailo Lomonosov*** among them

The Halshka Hulevychivna building — which now is a part of the Academy's campus — is ***the oldest residential building in Kyiv***

ar sciences were taught, along with ɔreign languages. The Collegium ·elcomed students from all strata of ociety. Upon Petro Mohyla's death, : was renamed the Kyiv Mohyla .cademy in honor of his unfailing upport for the institution. For some ime, the Academy was known as Mohylo-Mazepinska" — in honor f hetman Ivan Mazepa, who also upported the Academy and helped it expand by funding the construction of new buildings.

During the rule of the Tsars and the Soviets, the activities of the Academy were suspended. The University was restored in 1991 in an independent Ukraine. Today, the National University of Kyiv-Mohyla Academy, with its illustrious history and long-standing traditions, has over 3,000 students.

48

Taras Shevchenko National University of Kyi

The university is hard to miss — its impressive central building has a stunning red hue

Taras Shevchenko University opened to its inaugural class in 1834. At that time, it was named after St. Volodymyr and was located in rented premises in the Pechersk District. A well-known architect of Italian origin, Vincenzo Beretti, designed the majestic central building, and eight years after first opening the university campus was moved to theluxurious new building, pa ticularly impressive at that time because it had no surrounding buildings.

Why the red color? Well, that's a matter of debate. Some say that the paint ers simply made a mistake. The official version is that the walls are the color o the ribbons of St.Volodymyr's Order — red and black. In the post-war period, it was said that the red hue symbolized the blood that Ukrainian soldiers shed i defense of their country during the Second World War — a reminder that was meant to quell student protests at the time.

Today, over 26,000 students study at Taras Shevchenko University, specializing in one of almost a hundred different technical, natural science and humanities programs. Since 1939, the University has borne the name of Ukraine's greatest poet and artist, Taras Shevchenko.

Beretti founded a botanical garden near the Red Building — the site of over 9,000 plant species. Between 1908 and 1913, the garden also had a zoo

The University library is the ***largest academic library in Ukraine***. It has over 3.5 million books, including seven thousand unique antique books

eft page: The central building of the Taras Shevchenko National University of Kyiv
ight page: New buildings of the Taras Shevchenko National University of Kyiv

49

Khreshchatyk

It’s hard to imagine Kyiv without its main stree though it’s comparatively new for the ancient city — the first buildings were built in 1797

Where Khreshchatyk is today, there was originally a valley connecting the upper part of the city, Podil, and the Pechersk quarter. At the end of the eighteenth century a contract fair (a fair where all sorts of trade, marriage, or official contracts were signed) was held there, with a circus performance and folk dances and celebrations. Not long after, the area was actively developed — in 1876 the Kyiv city Duma was built there by the architect Alexander Shile, the main city developer of that period.

The same year saw the opening of the Grand Hotel National, which had twelve shops on its first floor, and ten years after that the Kyiv Stock Exchange opened. Ukraine’s first high-rise, Ginsburg House, was built on Khreshchatyk — this was the first eleven-story building in imperial Russia.

During the Second World War countless buildings on Khreshchatyk were blown up by the NKVD in the liberation of Kyiv from the Nazis. Others were burnt down in a firestorm. Khreshchatyk was also christened with a new German name during the war — Eichhornstrasse.

After the liberation of Kyiv in 1943, the people of the city began to clear up and rebuild the street. The following year, there was a competition for the

Khreshchatyk is 1.3km long and stretches between European Square and Bessarabska Square

The Ukrainian singer ***Pavlo Zibrov has a song dedicated to Kyiv's main street***

The first state telephone switchboard was built right on Khreshchatyk in 1886

est architectural projects to rebuild Khreshchatyk, with 22 entries for the
pen competition, and 11 entries for the private competition, held exclusively
or famous Soviet architects. Under the management of Kyiv's main archi-
ect, Anatoliy Dobrovolskyi, Khreshchatyk was given a modern look — a wide
horoughfare, flanked by chestnut trees and countless government buildings.

Today people flock to Khreshchatyk not only for its many shops but also
s recently developed TSUM department store. The street is closed to traffic on
ne weekends, and concerts and military parades are frequently held there.
he Maidan Square, which joins onto Khreshchatyk, became the main site for
kraine's two revolutions held during its independence — the Orange Revoluon, and the Revolution of Dignity, or Euromaidan.

50

The Motherland Monument

A female warrior stands guard over Kyiv

On Victory Day of May 9, 1981, the general secretary of the Communist Party — Leonid Brezhnev — unveiled "The Motherland". Original plans would have seen this monument gold-plated. But even the Soviet fondness for monumentalism had its limits, so the sculpture was fashioned instead out of stainless steel. Separate parts weighing several dozen tons each were welded at the Paris Commune plant in Kyiv.

In the end, the sculpture came to weigh around 450 tons. Together with its pedestal it reaches to 102 meters high. The steel woman brandishes a 9-ton sword in her right hand and 13-tonand 13×8-meter shield in her left.

Two elevators function inside of the sculpture. You can also climb the stairs up to the sword and shield where you'll find an observation deck.

"The Motherland" faces toward Moscow. Kyivans joke that she defends against Russians, a joke that has taken on new meaning during this time of war.

The Motherland Monument is a part of the Museum of the Great Patriotic War complex found at ***44 Ivan Mazepa Street***

51

Rusanivka

Kyiv's own "Little Venice" on an island in the Dnipro River

Rusanivka is a man-made island in Kyiv that was built out of four million cubic meters of sand. The Rusanivskyi Canal runs through the center of the island, as well as fifteen fountains, and it cuts the island off from the Left Bank of the city.

The whole development of Rusanivka only took ***thirteen years***

Rusanivka was designed as a model residential estate with its own infrastructure: each neighborhood has its own GP clinics, preschools, schools, parks, and shops. All of the buildings on Rusanivka Island are seventies-era high-rise blocks of flats, either 9 or 16 stories high.

Since the island was built up all at once, there's little chance of any new skyscrapers being built — only one new building has been built there since the '70s. There are three main streets on Rusanivka, which reduces the level of traffic and pollution there, and young families find it an attractive place to live.

Rusanivka's residents are known for their civic activism. hey actively follow up on the activities of local deputies and aise money for a civic budget to fund local projects, and have vebsites, online communities and forums dedicated to neighorhood issues.

Kyivites from other parts of the city as well as locals lock to Rusanivka's beaches. In summer, people from all ver come to relax and hang out by the water, or go for a amily walk in one of Rusanivka's many green spaces.

The actress ***Milla Jovovich*** lived in Rusanivka when she was a child

52

Crematorium

With its bold futurist design, you won't see another building like it

There were plans to build this crematorium in the 1960s, but they were continually put on hold to avoid any association with the infamous furnaces of the Nazi concentration camps during WWII, which remained a raw memory for many Kyivans. Eventually, the project was completed in 1975, based on a modern, futurist design by Ada Rybachuk and Volodymyr Melnychenko — the finished complex is called the Park of Commemoration.

Rybachuk and Melnychenko met during their studies at the Kyiv Institute of Art, and soon became inseparable, both in life and work. Upon researching everything there was to know about similar buildings in the history of world architecture, the young artists created a striking design — a genuine "Celestial Temple", as they called it.

Between the cemetery and the crematorium, Rybachuk and Melnychenko constructed a unique bas-relief Wall of Commemoration, which is 213 meters long between 4 and 14 meters tall. It took the artists 13 years to perfect the composition, which symbolizes the victory of life

Historian ***Mykhailo Hrushevskyii***, poetess ***Lesya Ukrainka***, and politician ***Volodymyr Shcherbytsky*** were laid to rest at Baikove Cemetary. Though it may seem somewhat morbid to visit a cemetery, its intricately carved headstones and sculptures make for a fascinating stroll

Ada Rybachuk and Volodymyr Melnyk also designed an incredible mosaic panel at Kyiv's Central Bus Station and the Palace of Children and Youth

ver death. An artificial lake was neant to be constructed nearby, so s to mirror the bas-relief. However, n 1982, Soviet authorities ordered he project (which was nearly completed at the time) to be drowned in concrete. The possibility of reviving this nasterpiece is still under discussion.

You can visit the Crematorium today on the Baikova Mount in the western part of the well-known Baikove Cemetery — Kyiv's necropolis. Ukraine's most famous scholars, scientists, artists, poets, sportsmen and public figures are buried at the Cemetery.

53

Tarilka

Near Lybidska metro station, Kyiv's "Tarilka" building (which translates as "plate") is a key example of Soviet Modernist architecture

Architect and painter Florian Yuriev was far ahead of his time when he created this daring project. Florian was born in Siberia, where his father was exiled. Having moved to Kyiv, Yuriev entered the Architecture Faculty of the Academy of Arts and took up painting, embracing a unique creative direction — the music of color. He even gave a concert where he played a color instrument, akin to a grand piano, causing the color gradients to fluctuate on the screen.

When the architect was entrusted with drawing a design for the Institute of SciTech and Economic Information, he decided to make the conference room of the building into an ideal venue for color-musical concerts. He worked on the project fastidiously until he was certain that sound would be distributed evenly across all 500 seats. This technical feat required that the conference room be shaped like a plate — it resembles a levitating UFO.

Yuriev received a USSR State Construction Committee Award for innovation in architecture for this design. Most of his successive projects were not so well received by Soviet authorities. Given this, he instead channeled his bubbling energy into other creative endeavors — he worked as a composer, musician, painter, sculptor, art critic and civil activist.

УКРІНТЕІ

Borshchahivka

A legacy of Soviet architecture and planning, today Borshchahivka is known for its own brand of chav culture and thuggery

Even the word "Borshchahivka" is associated with crime. This district of Kyiv lies far from the last subway lines: its industrial enterprises and factory dormitories mask a criminal underbelly.

The greatest risk for those who find themselves at Borshchahivka is meeting so-called *hopniki* — Ukrainian chavs — hooligans with shaved heads, and sports tracksuits (often counterfeits of well-known brands). The hopniks love *shansony* — music about crime and criminals. In pop culture, they're seen eating sunflower seeds while robbing random passersby, which in the vernacular is called a *hop stop*

he questionable culture of ***hopniks and hlobs*** (people with poor taste and little ulture) has inspired a group of Ukrainian rtists, who call themselves "zhlobologs"

Borshchahivka's twin is Troyeshchyna — a large residential area on the left bank of the Dnipro, which has the same ***dubious reputation***

Borshchahivka used to be a calm and cozy suburb of Kyiv, with lands elonging to city monasteries and small settlements. Nearby, Sviatoshyn — he neighborhood between Borshchahivka and the city center — was once n elite country district, a place of recreation for successful entrepreneurs, ocal artists and intellectuals.

Development in Borshchahivka took off in Soviet times, in 1966. To save unds, the development projects consisted of so-called *khrushchevky* (low-udget apartment buildings without elevators, and with tiny apartments) amed after Nikita Krushchev, and *gostinkas* (buildings with one-room otel-type apartments). These apartments were given out to the workers f local factories who hailed from all parts of Ukraine and the USSR.

55

Picturesque Alley

This quirky little alleyway in central Kyiv is a favorite spot for residents and visitors to experience Kyiv street life

In the 1980s, the city authorities began an ambitious architectural and historical project dedicated to restoring artifacts from Kyivan Rus. Just one project ended up being implemented — Picturesque Alley. This small street is located on the site of Kyiv's ancient defensive bulwarks. The Alley starts near the National Museum of History of Ukraine where the princes' palaces once stood, and passes along the foundation of Desiatynna Church — the first stone church in Kyiv. Prince Volodymyr built Desiatynna Church in 996. The church was destroyed in 1240 by the horde of Batu Khan.

In 2009, a park for children was added — with fantastic fountains shaped like elephants and zebras, huge cats, benches in the shape of hares and ravens, and other incredible sculptures. The project was designed by a young architect, Konstantyn Skrytutskyi, who decorated the alley with an art playground for children dedicated to the topic of economics.

One of Ukraine's oldest trees grows near the foundation of ***Desiatynna church*** — a linden tree. According to the legend, it was planted there by Petro Mohyla almost 400 years ago

The construction of the children's park cost about ***one million hryvnias***: 15 percent of the funds were raised by local residents, and the remainder was donated by businesses

From Picturesque Alley, a view opens to Vozdvyzhenska Street and s brightly colored buildings. Here, in Honchar-Kozhumiak district, ottery and tanning workshop workers once resided. Recently, Vozdyzhenska Street was rebuilt and the ancient spirit of the street was evived. Today, it's a favorite spot for wedding photos, weekend walks, nd art events.

56

Pyrohiv

You can go back in time with a visit to this vast open-air historical museum

Near the village of Pyrohiv, on the southern outskirts of Kyiv, you'll find the biggest open-air ethnographic museum in Europe. Here you can see over three hundred unique buildings from the sixteenth to the twentieth centuries. The museum opened for visitors in 1976, after its curators spent seven whole years collecting historical buildings from across Ukraine.

The National Museum of Folk Architecture and Life of Ukraine has residential houses from various regions of the country, windmills and watermills, churches, barns, a school, a tavern, a village council, and other buildings. Meandering through its pastoral grounds takes you back in time. If you take a guided tour, you'll be able to see many of the interiors of the buildings as well — giving you a sense of what life was like for peasants centuries ago.

Every weekend, the museum hosts various festivals where you can

The setting for the National Museum of Folk Architecture and Life of Ukraine is the bucolic countryside. You can spend the whole day here ***picnicking and exploring its numerous walking trails***

National holidays — Christian and ancient pagan alike — are observed at the Museum. Plan a visit during these times and join in the celebrations! To see what's on, go to: ***www.pyrohiv.com.ua/en***

The museum is also ***a popular place to get married***. Couples can choose to get married in one of a variety of churches from different regions of Ukraine

-arn national crafts from master -aftsmen, taste traditional dishes, -ıd enjoy Ukrainian singing and -ancing. The museum also occasionally organizes thematic exhibitions — there are over seventy thousand rare display pieces with unique icons, embroidery, dishes, and tools.

Funicular

The funicular has transformed from an essential mode of public transit into a real point of pride for the capital

As anyone wandering Kyiv's center will notice, it's a pretty hilly city. This has caused transportation problems for hundreds of years. The rise is particularly steep between lowland Podil and the center of the city, which is located on high hills.

Until the nineteenth century, the only way to get up to Mykhailivska Square was to take a long flight of wooden stairs. In 1892, the Russian Empire's first electric tramway opened in Kyiv, connecting the low and the high parts of the city, but it was a long, winding route, and very slow.

Around the same time, the Zurich-trained engineer Arthur Abrahamson came up with a novel idea: a mechanism on the hill based on Swiss elevators. By 1905, his vision

In 2013, Kyiv experienced major snowfall and the funicular took on a new use — as a ski lift. For a short spell, Volodymyr Hill and Andriyivskyi Descent became ***ski slopes***

'as realized. A 200-meter-long funicular railway connected
olodymyr Hill and Borychiv Tik Street.

In the middle of the 1930s, Soviet city builders decided
› move the funicular. They had plans to install decorative
:airs with a huge statue of Lenin at the top. The start of
ıe Second World War put a stop to these plans, and so the
ınicular was saved.

Today, the Kyiv funicular transports almost 3 million
assengers every year. The funicular cabin offers a fantastic
.ew of the Dnipro and of Trukhaniv Island. Catch a ride any
ay from 6 a.m. to 11 p. m — the three minute trip costs just
.ght hryvnias.

In Soviet times, the track was extended by almost *40 meters*

58

Salute Hotel

One of the most distinctive examples of Kyiv modernist architecture

Hotel Salute`s futuristic form resembles a spaceship coming down to land in Kyiv. In fact, the hotel's unusual look is caused by the abrupt junction of architectural ideas with the opinions of the authorities. According to the plans of architect Avraam Miletskyi, the building should have had 18 floors. However, the official commission that came from Moscow forbade the hotel from being built any higher — when it was only five stories high. The commission ruled that a building of that height would ruin Kyiv's historical panorama, although this panorama was later marred by residential complexes built nearby.

In order to save his design, Miletskyi worked out a new plan so that the hotel wouldn't look half-finished. Thi did end up significantly reducing the number of hotel rooms, and because of the impossibility of expansion, the hotel became very unprofitable.

Salute Hotel, as well as other modernist buildings, such as Floriar Yuriev's Tarilka building, the corpus of Kyiv University, designed by Mykhailo Budylovskyi, were attempt to turn the city into a living creative space, in contrast to the practice of building identikit buildings according to standard designs. However, Kyiv modernism was never fully realized as an artistic project. Instead, today these buildings remain as architectural moments which amaz and attract visitors to the city.

The Saliut Hotel is still running, and you can stay a night there. Just visit its official website *www.hotelsa-lute.ua/en*

59

Friendship of Nations Arch

This massive titanium arch in the center of the city is an ever-present reminder of Ukraine's complicated history with Russia

At Khreshchatyk Park a massive titanium arch looms over the right bank of the Dnipro. This monument was opened in 1982 on the anniversary of the October Revolution by the First Secretary of the Communist Party of Ukraine, Volodymyr Shcherbytskyi. It was meant to formally commemorate the "unification" of Russia and Ukraine, and the Friendship of Nations. But this "unification" was in fact achieved through protracted wars from 1917–1921, between Ukrainian forces representing the Ukrainian National Republic that declared independence in 1918, along with other Ukrainian governments, and the Bolshevik army of occupation from Russia. It took three attempts to establish Soviet rule in Ukraine.

In 1921–1923, as a result of draconian grain requisitions imposed by the Bolsheviks, a colossal famine broke out that claimed the lives of millions of people — a precursor to the more deadly famine, the Holodomor, of 1932–1933. The Ukrainian

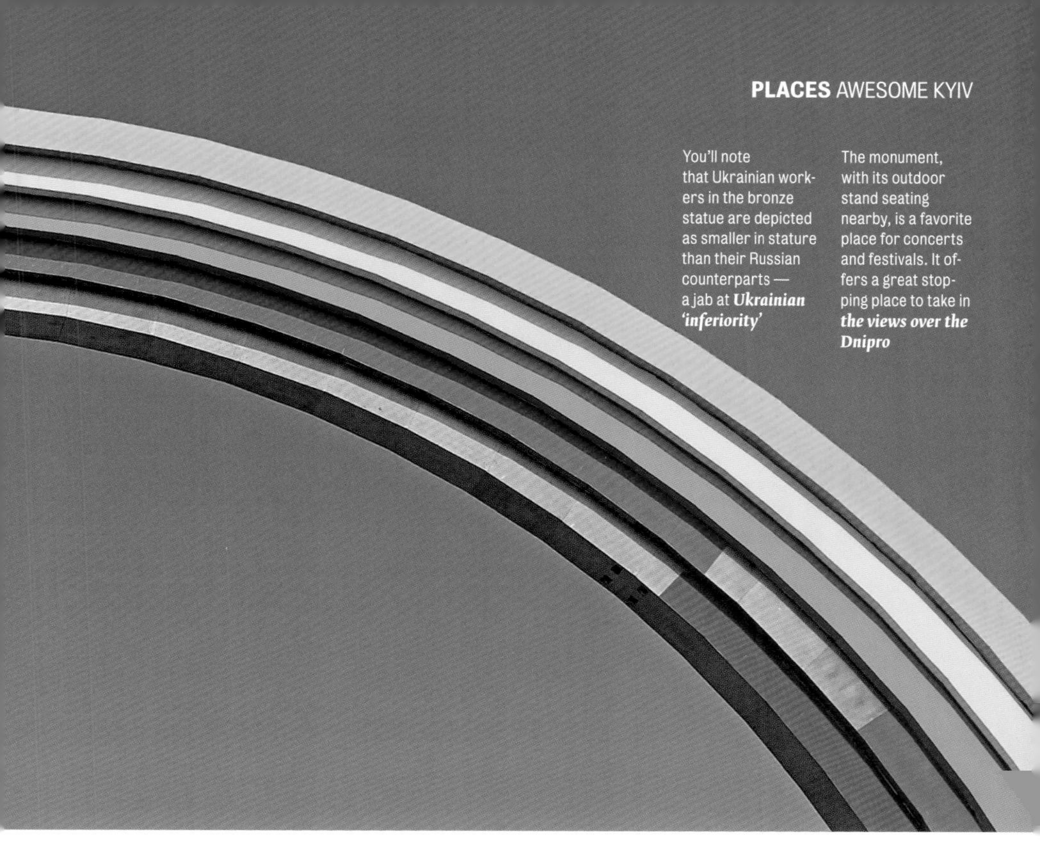

You'll note that Ukrainian workers in the bronze statue are depicted as smaller in stature than their Russian counterparts — a jab at ***Ukrainian 'inferiority'***

The monument, with its outdoor stand seating nearby, is a favorite place for concerts and festivals. It offers a great stopping place to take in ***the views over the Dnipro***

›viet Socialist Republic was formed . 1922 and became one of the con- ituent republics of the Soviet ıion. In Soviet propaganda, this cupation was always depicted as ı act of selfless friendship on the ırt of the Russian people. But in ct, it was a "unification" borne out war, famine and death.

The monument also includes a rge bronze statue of Russian and ‹rainian workers holding up the ›viet Order of Friendship of Peoples ong with a granite stele, depicting the participants of the Pereyaslav Council of 1654 (the Council convened by Bohdan Khmelnytsky to discuss Cossack hetmanate and Muscovy relations).

Although Russia and Ukraine have always been intimately bound, it is unclear what the future may hold. Today, as this text is being written, Russia has annexed Crimea and invaded the east of Ukraine: Russian forces are killing Ukrainians in an undeclared war. Ukrainians, now as ever, fight for their independence.

60

Metro

The city's arteries — the metro transports almost 1.5 million passengers daily

For a city of almost three million people, effective public transportation is a must. This fast and convenient public transit was supposed to appear in Kyiv at the end of the nineteenth century, when in 1884 the city council started considering designs for an underground railroad. They returned to this idea several times, but construction of the Metro started only after the Second World War. It was in 1960 that passengers were able to ride the first section of five stations — from Vokzalna to Dnipro — of the modern Sviatoshyno-Brovary line. In 1976, the second line opened — Kurenivsko-Chervnoarmiyska (during the construction, unique remnants of an ancient Kyivan Rus estate were found, bringing great joy to archaeologists), and in 1989, the third one, Syretsko-Pecherska, opened. Many of the earlier stations blend Stalinist architecture with Ukrainian motifs — each is architecturally unique and related to a specific theme. Later stations were much more functional in style.

Today, the Kyiv Metro's three lines cover 69,648 km. In all there are 52 stations with 122 functioning escalators. It takes less than 40 minutes to get from one end of Kyiv to the other. The designers plan to build three new lines and several new stations.

As Kyiv is a hilly city, some stations have an impressive depth. "Arsenalna" station is the deepest of these — its imposing escalators take you ***105.5 meters down***, a five-minute ride in all

A trip on the Metro will cost you less than ***50 American cents*** (8 Hryvnias). Tokens can be bought at any metro station

The mosaics at Palats Ukrayina metro station is now closed due to ***decommunization laws***

In its entire history, the Kyiv Metro was completely closed down only ıce — on February 18, 2014, due to the events during the Euromaidan Revoluon. The underground trains were shut down for around two days in an attempt prevent people from gathering on the Maidan, and the city ground to a halt.

Even during Soviet times, the announcements in the Metro were in krainian. Over the past 20 years, passengers have heard the voice of ykola Petrenko, the director of the Kyiv Academic Puppet Theater. English op announcements are voiced by an American announcer and professor, nthony Nox.

61

VDNG

All garish pomp and circumstance, Ukraine's Expocenter is a perfect example of Soviet neoclassical architecture

The construction of the National Expocenter of Ukraine, or VDNG (which stands for the Ukrainian for the Exhibition of the Achievements of the National Economy), began in 1952 and took six years to complete. There are 180 buildings in the Expocenter designed to show off the achievements of Soviet industry and agriculture. The pavilions held permanent exhibits on three main topics: Industry, Construction, and Transport; Agriculture; and Science and Culture; another pavilion was devoted to "visual agitation".

The Expocenter's architecture i unique: each of its buildings repre- sents differing architectural styles and decorations. The main pavilion have been recognized as architectu al landmarks, and in total, twenty buildings at VDNG have this status All the buildings' decorations glori- fy the Soviet regime and are covere in hammers and sickles.

After Ukraine's independence, the Expocenter fell upon hard

Parts of the comedy The Death of Stalin (2017) were shot on the Kyiv Expocenter's grounds. Nikita Khrushchev, who was the ideological inspiration for the real VDNG, was played by Steve Buscemi

Every year, ***the summer festival Atlas Weekend is held at VDNG.*** Bands such as Kasabian, The Killers, The Prodigy and The Chemical Brothers have performed at the festival

imes. Eventually it came to be ısed again, and not just as an xhibition space. Today various hows and events are held there, uch as the Winter Country Fair, vith ice skating and an ice-sculpture park, the 3D fairy-tale show *Varlock Dreams*, the Atlas Weekend nusic festival, the Kurazh Bazaar lea market, a tattoo festival, and craft beer festival. The Expocenter also has a swimming pool, a horse-riding school, children's playgrounds, a ropes course, and various bike rentals.

Thanks to all of this, VDNG now has the status of a cultural and entertainment complex, which, instead of expos on tractors, courgettes, and seeds, brings together all sorts of cultural initiatives and projects.

Bursa

A small boutique hotel with 33 cozy bedrooms, a rooftop bar, an intimate library, and an independent art gallery

The Bursa concept is nurtured by the local creative community, those who are building their future, freedom of expression and happiness. Everyone here is welcome to be themselves. Founded in 2018, Bursa has already become a meeting point for like-minded people from all over the world.

Bursa finds itself right on the crossroads of history and youth culture, in the very center of Podil, Kyiv's historical but vibrant neighborhood. The neoclassical building that now houses Bursa was once the home of Andrey Melensky, Kyiv's first chief architect. The project and interior design were created by Balbek

The inspiration for the neon phrases found scattered round the hotel — suc as ***"Three word are two words"* or *"Dance for me, Tolya"*** — comes from bits of graffiti found elevators in Kyiv

Bursa is located at ***11 Kostiantynivska Street***

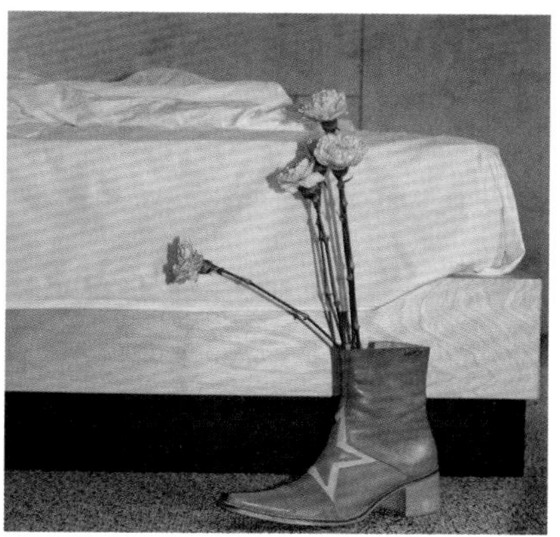

ureau. The design concept is the combination of the austerity of aw, uncovered constructions and the softness of a cozy, laid-back tmosphere. "The main idea running through the entire design is auhaus-style principles," says Slava Balbek, leading architect.

Following the "less is more" principle of minimalistic esign, Bursa appreciates the aesthetics of simplicity while voiding making things boring. That's why the interior is lled with color accents, art and humor. The combination of istorical and modern details underlines coexistence of past nd present in one space.

Many years ago ***a huge old chestnut tree grew on the territory of the Bursa.*** Unfortunately, it was cut down for unknown reasons. So the Bursa team decided to plant a new one, that you can see at the yard

63

Circus

The Kyiv Circus is still a popular attraction, though it might be ethically questionable to use animals in its performances

Kyiv's dome-topped round circus is part of a long tradition of revelry in the city. Before the first stationary circus opened, fairs provided the main entertainment for Kyivans. One of the most renowned was Kontraktovy Fair, which opened in 1797, providing city dwellers with performances by wandering *skomorokhs* — jugglers, acrobats, actors, minstrels, conjurors, and musicians.

Kyiv's circus use to be the site of a unique church built of iron — ***t John Chrysost*** (Ioan Zolotoust) church. The church was dismantled by th Soviet government in 1934, ye the name of the nearby street, Zlatoustivska, reminds us of its legacy

Kyiv's first permanent circus building appeared in 1875, on the location of the Lesia Ukrainka Modern Theater of Russian Drama. Later, a local businessman launched a competing institution, where the brightest stars of entertainment

r a long time, the Nikitin brothers' Kyiv
cus hosted performances of the six-
ne world champion in wrestling,
an Piddubny

Pavlo Skoropadskyi was elected hetman in the Krutikov circus building during
the revolt of 1918

erformed, including wrestlers, acrobatic cyclists, and tam-
rs. In 1903, Peter Krutikov's Horse Circus, Hippo-Palace,
pened — with its 2,000 seats, it was the largest in Europe.
his building was the pride of Kyivans until 1941, when it
vas demolished by the retreating Soviet troops.

Architect Valentyn Zhukov, who built circuses in several
ther Soviet cities, designed the modern Kyiv Circus at 2 Pere-
nohy Square in 1960. The circus can hold an audience of around
,000 people. It's used for both classic and experimental perfor-
nances, like the recent "Circus on Water" performance.

In 2017 a series of protests ***"Circus without animals"*** was started and continue until now and become more popular

The Naked Room

A contemporary art gallery, founded in 2018 by two curators along with a film director

The Naked Room is an art gallery, founded by curators Lizaveta Herman, Mariia Lanko and Marc Wilkins. There are no restrictions on age or genre for the artists on display at the Naked Room, and alongside art exhibitions the gallery holds lectures, film viewings, and pop-up events, brought together by the Naked Statement outfit.

The gallery also shares a space with the Naked Bar, set up by Foodies, a group of gastro-aficionados. It also has a book corner run by IST Publishing. The bookshelves are stocked specially by the curators of the gallery, choosing volumes on art, photography, and publishing from over 15 countries. Books can either be purchased or are available for guests to leaf through with a cup of coffee at the bar.

The Naked Room is located at ***21 Reitarska Street***, and open everyday from 11 am to 8 pm

Reitarska Street was also specially chosen for its dynamic place on the yiv scene, with parties and events taking place all the time, and with ew cultural spaces and creative businesses opening there.

65

Kyiv River Port

Daily from April to November — from the first sunny days to the first frosts — you can go on river tours of the Dnipro

Kyiv River Port and Boat Station (Richkovyi vokzal) is situated on the Dnipro's Right Bank, in the historical part of the city, Podil. The construction of the port took nearly 10 years and was finished in 1961.

The towers of the building are shaped like a ship's masts, and the station's interior is decorated with mosaics by Ukrainian artists Ernest Kotkov, Valerii Lamakh, and Ivan Lytovchenko.

In the summer season, tours of the Dnipro set off from the River Station, which allows you to explore the whole of Kyiv for roughly $15-$20. The river port also provides for another interesting mode of public transport — the river tram, which connects the Left and Right banks of Kyiv. The boats can also be rented for events upon request. For example, students at the Kyiv-Mohyla Academy arrange themed parties on them, called *korablyky*.

Walking tours have departed from Kyiv River Station for over 25 years. You can book an excursion on the official website ***www.rpea.com.ua***

66

Kyiv Cycle Track

Not just any old cycle track — Kyiv's Velodrome is integral to the city's sport and culture

Over a hundred years ago, upon the initiative of Kyivite Ivan Bilenko, a "cycledrome" was built in the recently filled-in Afanasivskyi Yar. Here you could rent and repair bicycles, cars, and motorcycles. Over the years, the track has been surfaced with various materials — at first with tarmac, then concrete, and then in the 1980s it was covered with wood.

In 2006, the land which the velodrome stands on was sold for development, and after its partial demolition one part of the track was made into high-rise flats. Activists struggled to save the sports complex, but only managed to get government support in 2014. The Kyiv Association of Cyclists (now called U-Cycle) playe an integral role in this turnover.

The restored cycling track had it opening ceremony in the spring of 2017. Since then, the Velodrome has functioned as a free cycling school for children and a sports hall, and it has parking and seats for spectators Employees at the Velodrome give fre cycling lessons and allow anyone to practice on the track — provided they have the right equipment. You'll often see amateur racing and cycle-polo competitions; runners

The Velodrome has had ***an outdoor theater with an orchestra***, the Poliarna Zirka ("Pole Star") since its opening in 1912. A year later, a cinema booth also appeared, and films were shown open air, directly on the track

In order to popularize cycling in Ukraine, the organisation U-Cycle holds promotional events such as ***the Bike to Work and Girls Cycle Parade campaigns***, and it also runs a school on cycle safety

so often train here, and kids often ay on rollerblades on the track. owever, you'll see the majority of ople at the velodrome are there for the photo opportunity (although we could argue that any representation of cycling on Instagram increases interest in the sport).

NATURE

Right page: The chestnut tree — the unofficial ***symbol of Kyiv***

67

Dnipro River

Flowing from Russia to the Black Sea, it is the fourth longest river in Europe

This life-giving river has a long and varied history. Dnipro means "Great River" — and great it is, flowing for over 2,200 km through three countries, providing water and electricity to several densely-populated cities along the way.

Herodotus mentioned the Dnipro long ago, in the fifth century BC. The Greeks called the river Borysthenes and believed that it had a river god-patron of the same name. Ancient Eastern Slavs called the river Slavutych (this name was given, later, to a town on the riverbank, a subway station in Kyiv, and also to numerous commercial brands). Back in the times of Kyivan Rus, the Dnipro served as a main transportation artery, connecting the Black and the Baltic Seas. Chroniclers referred to this route as "the great way from the Varangians to the Greeks." Later on, the banks of the Dnipro were home to the famous Zaporizhzhian Sich.

Up until a hydro power station was constructed in the 1960s, the Dnipro was simultaneously a source of life and a terrible threat – every spring the river flowed over its banks and flooded some districts of the city. Now, since the river's been tamed, it's a favorite place to relax and swim.

Dnipro is a popular brand name locally — borne by a football club, a rocket carrier, a motorcycle, a publishing house, a hotel, a subway station, and numerous other things in Kyiv and Ukraine

68

Chestnuts

If Tokyo attracts tourists with cherry blossom, one comes to Kyiv in the spring to see the blooming chestnut trees

Every May, white and pink “candles” bloom on almost every city street, turning the noisy metropolis into a fragrant garden. Couples stroll the boulevards, and the city comes alive after the long winter months. Short skirts appear and Kyiv’s “flâneurs” put Parisians to shame.

This lush canopy has become so synonymous with Kyiv that it’s hard to imagine the streets without them — but they are a relatively new addition, planted in the nineteenth century. It is said that General Bibikov introduced the trees to the streets of Kyiv in preparation for a visit by Emperor Nikolai I. The then-exotic trees were planted on every newly-built street (such as Taras Shevchenko Boulevard) in an effort to impress the royal visitor. However, the trees were all dug up and replaced with poplars the night before the emperor’s visit, by order of the governor-general. Apparently, the emperor had grimaced when Bibikov’s messenger mentioned the chestnut trees, in describing the reception ceremony awaiting him — which lead to the late-night tree switch. But this was all for naught. It was later revealed that Nikolai had actually grimaced because of a passing bumblebee.

The oldest chestnut tree in Kyiv grows in Kytaivska Retreat, near Troitska Church. It's about *300 years old, 15 meters high, and almost four meters in girth*! According to legend, it was planted by Metropolitan Petro Mohyla

In 1982, municipal authorities discussed what date to choose to celebrate the day of Kyiv. They decided on *the last Sunday of May* when Kyiv is in its finest form, as the chestnut trees are in full bloom

Luckily, the planting stock of ıestnut trees was saved by Kyiv niversity students, who replant- ı them in the nearby botanical arden. And from the garden, the ıestnut trees spread across the city.

In the Soviet Era, Kyiv's city emblem was a design of a chestnut leaf and blossom. Today, chestnut trees are the city's unofficial symbol.

Maryinskyi Park

A walk in one of the capital's loveliest parks was once an elite privilege — accessible only to members of the tsar's family

Founded in 1874, Maryinskyi Park was formerly known as Dvortsovyi Park ("park of the palace"). It's situated opposite the Maryinskyi Palace, which served as a residence for the leaders of the Russian Empire.) Presently, it's mostly used as a venue for State ceremonial events. Emperor Alexander II's wife, Maria, actively endorsed the construction of the Park. That's why, some years later, it was re-named Maryinskyi Park — in her honor. Decorative trees and shrubs were planted, and later on, an exquisite cast-iron fountain was installed. The fountain was produce

e Park boasts over *80 tree species*, in-
ıding some rare ones, like the Kentucky
ffeetree, the ailanthus, and the Japa-
se pagoda tree

There is *a Lovers' Bridge* in Maryinskyi Park. If you "lock" your love to its railings, it's thought that your love will be eternal

t a Kyiv plant founded by the engi-
eer and inventor Oleksii Termen (a
elative of Lev Termen, theinventor
f an electronic musical instrument
alled a termenvox).

Maryinskyi Park offers breath-
aking views of and beyond the Dni-
ro River from its observation deck.
s you stroll the Park, you'll come
cross a Water Museum located in a
ineteenth century water tower, a
airytale palace that houses the Kyiv
cademic Puppet Theater, a small amphitheater, as well as an array of sculptures and monuments, such as a bronze statue of renowned poetess Lesya Ukrainka.

During the Euromaidan Revolution, Maryinskyi Park was used as a campsite for so-called anti-Maidan activists, who left trampled grass, broken benches and lanterns, and heaps of garbage behind. Kyiv residents volunteered to clean up and repair the Park — restoring it to its former beauty.

70

Trukhaniv Island

A summer resort town in the very heart of the city

Kyiv is a city with real seasons, and in the summer Trukhaniv Island comes alive. It's situated on the Dnipro River, just offshore from Podil. Trukhaniv Island has a long history. It was named after the Kuman Khan Tugor Khan. At the end of the eleventh century, his daughter (who later became the wife of Prince Sviatopolk of Kyiv) took up residence on the island.

By the end of the 1930s, Trukhaniv Island was home to over 7,000 city dwellers and had a school, a church and 367 resi-

Trukhaniv Island has a functionin
36-meter tall parachute tow

ential buildings. All structures were built on high wooden iles due to spring flooding. When flooded, residents would et around in boats, leading to the nickname "Kyivan Venice". 1 1943, the Nazi invaders completely burned down the settle-nent as they fled in retreat.

Postwar, the island was dedicated to recreation. It was a opular spot. Kyivans used to wait in long lines for a crowded oat to take them from Podil to the island. In 1957, all this hanged when a walking bridge was built. With the construc-on of Kyiv's hydroelectric dam in 1964, the island's problems ith flooding were no more.

Trukhaniv Island is a little oasis in the middle of bustling yiv. It's an ideal location for bicycle rides, picnics, sunbath-ng, water-skiing and wakeboarding.

Poet *Lina Kostenko* spent her childhood on the Island. Her poem "I grew up in Kyiv Venice" is dedicated to these years of her life

71

Lysa Hora

This mystical mountain is a favorite hangout for local Tolkien fans, goths, geeks, Satanists and, well, pretty much everybody

Ancient Ukrainians referred to treeless mountains as "bald" mountains. It was said that they looked that way because lightning had hit them — a sign of mystical forces at work. These spiritually intriguing places, with their attachment to another realm, became a site for pagan rituals. The introduction of Christianity changed all this. The mystical mountains were instead viewed as cursed places where witches and other evil forces gathered for their Sabbath or held orgies with demons.

In the nineteenth century, the so-called Lysohirskyi Fort was built here — a branch of the Kyiv Fortress. Soldiers on evening patrol were forewarned that they shouldn't be spooked by eerie noises. But the mountain got the best of some of them... insanity and suicide were frequent. From 1906 on political prisoners were executed a the fort and buried on the slopes o the mountain.

With this kind of history and folklore it's hardly surprising that

According to legend, after taking Kyiv in 1240, Batu Khan sealed the entrances to caves under Lysa Hora. Thousands of Kyivans who had taken refuge there are said to have perished in agony

In Soviet times, Lysa Hora was home to jamming stations that prevented American and European radio broadcasts from reaching Kyivans

Despite its gruesome history, Lysa Hora is said to be lucky — they say if you make a wish atop the mountain, it will come true

yiv's Lysa Hora (literally "Bald ountain") is a favorite hang-out r local Tolkien fans, historic enactors, Goths and geeks. The ountain's macabre history and ıcient mythology have been a ırticular draw for local Satanists ıd neopagans, who are known hold ceremonies there. A pagan mple with wooden idols can be found on Lysa Hora even today — it's a favorite spot during the ten-day Slavic pagan celebration Grudie Rosnoe.

Since 1982, Lysa Hora has been a nature park open for visitors — it's a lovely place for a quiet stroll, just steps from the bustling city. Its great views over Podil make it a popular destination for all sorts of visitors.

72

Lybid River

This time-honoured Kyiv River is now hidden underground

This small tributary of the Dnipro, named after Lybid, the sister of the founders of Kyiv, once had its source in the Solomianskyi district of Kyiv. In the times of Kyivan Rus it was a deep river — various vessels used it for navigation, watermills were located here, and bream and crucian carps, caught in the river, were considered the tastiest in the city. For a long time it was also Kyiv's natural border.

Many Kyiv rivers have survived to our day only in the chronicles o names of adjace streets: like *Pochaina, Syre and Hlybochyts*

All this changed with industrialization in the nineteenth century. New plants and factories proliferated and discharged their waste into the river. The Lybid grew polluted, and spring floods wreaked havoc. In the twentieth century, the river was covered over and hidden underground. While the Lybid is around 14 km long, today the river flows along its natural riverbed for only half a kilometer. You can see the Lybid exiting the sewer from Lysa Hora. The Lybid disgorges into the Dnipro near the Southern Bridge and before doing so, is greeted by numerous small tributaries that once were an important part of Kyiv, like the Shuliavka or Protasiv Yar.

The Khresh-chatyk, a small tributary of the Lybid, flows underneath the main street of the capital, which bears the same name. The river was rechanneled underground at the end of nineteenth century due to regular flooding

73

Pushcha-Vodytsia Tram

In just one hour you can go from a residential area in the heart of Kyiv to an idyllic forest — just hop on the no. 12 tram

Kyivans love to get out and enjoy the countryside, and Pushcha Vodytsia is a much-loved destination. Its dense forests, located on the northwestern outskirts of the capital, have long been a place to relax and enjoy the outdoors. During Kyivan Rus, the area was a hunting ground favored by princes. By the end of the nineteenth century, it was developed into a recreational area. People started to build dachas and recreation facilities on the land. This forced municipal authorities to tackle the issue of transport and communication. In 1900, rails were laid between Kontraktova Square and Pushcha-Vodytsia, and a so-

The tram route between Kontra tova Square and Pushcha-Vodyts is the longest in Kyiv — *almost kilometers long* The ride takes one hour and 12 minutes to complete and makes 40 stops along the way

alled "locomobile" — a steam tram — was established; after
ur years it was upgraded to an electrical tram.

The new rail route made travel to the area more comfort-
ble. But it also proved to be a critical infrastructure link
uring the First and Second World Wars: the tram was used to
ansport wounded soldiers, and delivered firewood for heat-
g during the dead of winter.

There is yet another tram route you can use to access
ushcha-Vodytsia: the no.7, which starts in Obolon, at Taras
hevchenko Square. This tram takes only half an hour to get
 the final stop — a cozy park with huge oak trees and pines,
clear pond, sports grounds and beaches. No need to be in a
urry to get there: the tram ride through the majestic forest is
pleasure in itself.

From Obolon to Pushcha-Vodytsia, you can take *a retro-tram for group excursions*. The trams are identical to the ones used in Kyiv in 1892, both inside and out. The retro tram was a labor of love; tram car enthusiasts refurbished it from old spare parts in 2006

74

Lake Telbyn

Kyiv is a city of lakes — it has over 100 of them

Kyivans relish being surrounded by picturesque lakes, the majority of which are clean and you can bathe in them. Welcoming lakeshores are transformed into beaches, with boat rentals, playing pitches and playgrounds, cafes and restaurants, picnicking areas, and shops lining them.

The biggest lake in Kyiv is Lake Telbyn (1.8 sq km). Residents from the neighboring Berezniaky District make great use of it. The deepest lake is Tiahle Lake in the Darnytsia District. Its depth was increased by 30 meters when its bottom was dredged for sand, used in a construction project nearby. In Darnytsia there's a lake teeming with over 30 fish species. Among them you can even find the endangered goby fish. Babyne Lake on Trukhaniv Island features incredible plants. Meanwhile Synie (Blue) Lake at Vynohradar is considered the cleanest. Some even believe that its waters have healing properties.

The left bank of the Dnipro has more lakes than the right, and they are wider and deeper than the right-bank ones. This is because *the sand left bank was once covered by the Dnipro*

SPORTS

The Death Match

One of the most popular sports legends of Soviet times

This legend takes place in 1942. The story goes that Nazi invaders in occupied Kyiv learned of some soccer players from the local team Dynamo. They decided to arrange a show match to profile their own team's football prowess — which was renowned in Europe at the time. Kyiv's hungry and tired football players were reputedly forewarned: lose the match or lose your life. Instead, the former Dynamo players beat the team of invaders with a devastating score of 5:0. The Nazis did not forgive such impudence. Come night, they arrested the team, drove them to Babyn Yar and had them executed.

The Soviet press exploited this heroic story for many generations. The well-known writer Lev Kassil dubbed the event the "Death Match." The reality, however, was a bit different.

The 2012 Russian film The Match is based on The Death Match legend. In Ukraine, there was a scandal during the movie's release. The movie contains a heavy dose of Russian propaganda: Ukrainians in the movie were depicted as Nazi-collaborators, while Russians were depicted as heroic

There are three ***memorials to the soccer players of Start*** in Kyiv — at the Dynamo Stadium, at the Start Stadium, and one near the place where the Syretskyi concentration camp was located

Kyiv Dynamo's football players vere not conscripted — to survive, hey ended up working at a baking factory. In their free time they racticed at the local Zenit Stadim. The German authorities — who vanted to restore the cultural and ports life in occupied Kyiv — were uite accepting of the sportsmen's nitiative and even helped to organse a series of matches.

During this improvised soccer eason, the team Start (consisting of players from Dynamo and Locomotive) devastated a team from the German anti-air unit Flakelf. The anti-air unit team retaliated, but Start emerged victorious again — with a score of 5:3. Players were arrested within days of the match; most team members were sent to concentration camps, and four soccer players were executed. But some historians don't see a direct correlation between their victory and their death.

FC Dynamo

The internationally renowned Dynamo is Ukraine's most sucessful and popular football club

It is the most titled club, not only in Ukraine, but in the entire former Soviet Union. The club's achievements include dozens of Cups and Super Cups in national and USSR championships, a UEFA Super Cup and two Cup Winners' Cups.

FC Dynamo Kyiv was founded in 1927 and was then known for its "Chekist" affiliations. "Chekists" were members of the Soviet Union's first state security organisation. Despite professionalization over the years, the club maintained connections with the state security apparatus until the collapse of the USSR.

In the 1990s, Kyiv Dynamo became privately owned by Hryhoriy Surkis. Some of the club's most notable players include Serhiy Rebrov, Andriy Shevchenko, Leonid Buriak, and Oleh Blokhin, who played 586 matches and scored 270 goals for Dynamo. No mention of Dynamo would be complete without honoring its most prominent coach —

As part of the Soviet Union until its collapse in December 1991, the club has also won ***13 USSR Championships, 9 USSR Cups, and 3 USSR Super Cups,*** making Dynamo the most successful club in the history of the Soviet Top League

lleriy Lobanovskyi (1939–2002). He as elected head coach thrice and l the team to win the Cup Winners' Cup twice. Dynamo's main rival clubs are FC Arsenal Kyiv (Kyiv derby) and Shakhtar (Donetsk).

77

Valeriy Lobanovskyi

Valeriy Lobanovskyi began his professional football career with FC Dynamo Kyiv in 1957

Though he only played for the club for five years, his name is forever associated with it. At the age of twenty-nine, Lobanovskyi left his football career to take the position of coach for Dnipropetrovsk FC Dnipro. Within five years he returned to Dynamo in this role. Shortly after becoming coach he introduced his signature tactical approach to training and led the team to become the number one football team in the USSR and winners of the UEFA Winners Cup and Super Cup.

Valeriy Lobanovskyi was three times elected head coach of the USSR football team and three times became Dynamo head coach. He dedicated many years to the club. Under Lobanovskyi's coaching, Dynamo won the Cu Winners' Cup twice, the championsh of the USSR eight times and the Cup o the USSR six times!

After a period of absence, Valeriy Lobanovskyi returned to Dynamo in 1997 to lead his native club to the UEFA Champions League semifinals, giving him a new chance to enter the "high society" of European football.

After Valeriy Lobanovskyi's death in May 2002, Dynamo — having lost its mentor — failed to win the Championship of Ukraine for t very first time.

Following his death, Lobanovskyi was awarded the title *Hero of Ukraine*, the nation's highest honor. Dynamo Kyiv's Stadium was renamed the Lobanovskyi Stadium in his honor

Vitali and Volodymyr Klitschko

Heavyweight boxing champions

These brothers — Vitali (born in 1971) and Volodymyr (born in 1976) — have taken the boxing world by storm. After Volodymyr's victory at the Olympics in Atlanta (1996), the brothers started their professional careers under the supervision of German trainer Fritz Zdunek. From their first victories by knockout, they proved to be very dangerous opponents. Starting in 1998, these prominent boxers hav been determinedly taking the belts the most authoritative boxing assoc ations from the world's best boxers.

ali Klitschko is presently ***the Mayor of iv*** and was a prominent political figure ring Ukraine's Euromaidan Revolution. holds a PhD in Sports Science

Volodymyr Klitschko, is ***the WBA (Super), IBF, WBO, IBO and The Ring World Heavyweight Champion***

On June 2, 2011, after Volody-ıyr Klitschko's victory over British avid Haye, the brothers — having nited their accomplishments — ecame owners of champion belts ı the heavyweight category of the ur most prestigious internation- boxing organizations.

Vitali and Volodymyr are not just exceptional sportsmen — they have brawn and brains! Both brothers are involved in politics and philanthropy and are avid chess players. Vitali has put his boxing career aside and is currently the Mayor of Kyiv.

79

Deriugina School

Ukrainian gymnasts are amongst the best in the world, thanks to the legendary coaches Albina and Iryna Deriugina

Ukrainian gymnasts are world-famous. They took the sporting world by storm in the 1970s as part of the USSR team.

At the time, Albina Deriugina was a lead coach of the female athletes. Her daughter Iryna achieved considerable success under her mother's guidance. She was twice world champion (in 1977 and in 1979), and after retirement she followed in her mother's footsteps and also became a coach.

Together, this impressive mother-daughter duo founded a calisthenics school, which went on to produce many sports stars. The graduates of the Deriuginas'

Since 1992, the School has held the ***Deriugina Cup competitions*** — the most prestigious calisthenics contest in Ukraine

:hool include world champions — :hletes like Hanna Bezsonova, leksandra Tymoshenko, Oksana :aldina, Tamara Yerofeyeva, and atalia Hodunko. For a time, the :hool trained Kateryna Serebrian- :a and Olena Vitrychenko. Ath- tes from Japan, Norway, Finland ıd other countries flocked to the :hool to train.

During the late 2013-early 2014 Euromaidan-protest in Kyiv, the school changed training halls several times, and their main training center, the October Palace became occupied by protesters.

Today, the Kyiv School of Rhythmic Gymnastics has several branches across the city where top coaches supervise young female athletes.

80

Kachalka

This outdoor gym in Kyiv's Hydropark is "the most hardcore in Europe"

If Mad Max had a gym, it would look like Kachalka. The gym is located in Hydropark – a waterfront entertainment park with beaches and attractions on Kyiv's Venetian and Dolobetskyi Islands in the Dnipro River. These islands have a long history, with settlements predating Kyivan Rus. Durin the Second World War the islands were laid to waste, and after the war it was decided that they should be transformed into a recreation area for Kyivans. The park formally opened in the 1960s and was an instant hit.

The park was improved by Yuriy Kuk, a professor of mathematics, who worked in the Cybernetics Institute at the National Academy of Sciences. Together with Polish gymnast Kazimir Yagelski, he started to add gym equipment. It all began with a bar set between two trees. Later old tires, fragments of pipes, radiators, automotive parts from waste dumps, and wooden planks were added – and Kachalka gym was born.

For many years, Kachalka lost fitness machines to thieves, who stole parts to sell as scrap metal. To prevent this, the machines have been fixed on the spot with chains, giving the site even more of ***a post-apocalyptic look***

Kachalka gained notoriety when Ukrainian photographer ***Kirill Golovchenko*** published a collection of photographs titled Kachalka. Muscle Beach dedicated to this location

Today in Kachalka you'll find over 150 fitness machines spread over ***10,000 square meters***

This outdoor, cobbled-together gym has been built up gradually over
.e years, and just keeps growing in popularity. Anyone can train here
r free. It attracts schoolchildren, pensioners, men, women, pros and
nateurs... pretty much everyone. Its outdoor location makes it an ideal
ace for bodybuilders to show off, and gawkers to gawk.

81

Chess Players

There are a spot in Kyiv's central Shevchenko park where dozens of chess players come to meet and play against each other

"Sadochok" — meaning "little garden" — is one of Shevchenko Park's real treasures. Located in the southern corner of the park, it is predominantly populated by a contingent of elderly aficionados of chess, draughts, and other table games. You can see them nearly all year round, since they only tend to take a break in the coldest months. Anyone can come and have a look, but if you want to play a game with one of the regulars, you'll have to prove your skills and earn their trust.

Most of the chess players here look like amateurs, yet many of them have played in serious championships. Sometimes chess grandmasters even come to play in Sadochok. Hence you shouldn't be surprised if you are beaten in a matter of minutes — these pros train every day. Although the stakes are not as high as they used to be, it is said that

In the sixties, *card players used to meet on a square b Zoloti Vorota,* but when some embassy buildi were built on nearby streets they were clea out. They move on to Shevche park, where th were joined by chess players, and devotees of draughts an backgammon

Soviet times some players managed to earn up to several ousand roubles in a day. Some of the old men playing here ke a break from playing and rent their boards for people ho want to play a game with friends — although for forgners the price is a little higher, of course.

Today, Sadochka's visitors are worried about its fate — ot just that there are fewer and fewer serious games being ayed here, but that they can even be driven out of their loved hangout.

In any case, in summertime there's no point trying to nd a table to play on — players come out in droves in the arm weather in order to spend a day playing chess or other mes underneath the shade of the trees.

There are rumours that in the turbulent years of the nineties, two 'katals' (scam artists in the gambling business) won over 100,000 dollars from people, and *one doctor lost so much money that he had to sell his house and country dacha, in order to pay off his debts*

82

River Fun

When there's good weather in the city, a kayak trip might be just the ticket for more active-minded people

Between the Dnipro and the Rusanivskyi Strait, Hidropark Island has all sorts of beaches, places for boat hire, canoes, and other water sports.

There is indeed quite a lot to choose from, although we can recommend renting a kayak and exploring the dozens of beaches on the island and going round the island itself. You can see things whilst on the water that are hidden from the shore, and also explore little channels around the island.

Kayaking isn't particularly difficult, although if you are uneasy using one for the first time, you can hire a two-person kayak and go on in with an instructor or another person

You can also rent kayaks in other parts of the city, such as ***Slavutych, Obolon, and Berezniaky***

ou trust. In addition, the hire center is located in a closed rea of the river where motorboats and others boats aren't llowed to enter, though it still has an exit onto the Dnipro.)f course, before they let you out onto the water, you must o through an induction and be instructed on how to act in mergency situations.

Real extremists can try out kayaking not just in the ummer but in the winter too — but you'll need special quipment for this.

To find out more details about renting a kayak at the hire center's official website *www.kayakcenter.com.ua*

83

Protasiv Yar

Kyivans don't need to leave the city to visit a ski resort — they have their very own

Kyiv's long winter months are buoyed by the capital's centrally located ski resort, Protasiv Yar. You can rent equipment onsite and ski down one of four routes — from simple training routes for children and beginners, to the extreme professional one. The ski resort even has a snowboard park. Here one can find a park for snowboarders with jumps and rails. The park makes use of artificial snow — prolonging the seasons from November to April, regardless of the weather.

While the resort is beloved by loca skiers and snowboarders, it's also of interest to archeologists. The history of this location dates back to Trypillia culture. Nestled between two hills (Batyi and Baikova), the site is named after the wealthy General Protasov, who owned the nearby village. At the beginning of the twentieth century, Protasiv Yar became part of Kyiv, and i became an industrial zone.

Protasiv Yar regularly holds city and oblast sports events. In 2001, the European Cup in snowboarding was held here.

ı summer, ***adren-line junkies fly 'own the hills*** f Protasiv Yar in zorbas" — trans-arent inflatable alls full of air

The slopes are lit up ***every Saturday*** for those who love skiing at night

84

Olympic Stadium

The country's main sports arena sits nestled into one of the central hills in Kyiv

Ukraine's National Sports Complex — the Olympic Stadium — first opened in 1923. In true Soviet form it was called "Red Stadium" at the time. Its fantastic location adds to its atmosphere — it is situated in the centrally located Alekseevskyi Park, near the base of Cherepanova Mountain. The mountain's slopes were utilized in the construction of the stadium's stands. Not long after opening, the Stadium was renovated. Its reopening was going to be celebrated with a Dynamo Kyiv football match on June 22, 1941, until WWII broke out on that very same day. From that day forward, major sporting events would be postponed for years to come.

The National Sports Complex "Olympic Stadium" has ***a histor museum*** where you'll find many unique objects — from photograph and sports trophies to items from the private collections of fan

In 1966 the Stadium was again renovated, and for a time it had the largest capacity of any stadium in the Soviet Union and Europe. Kyiv's Stadium held seven football matches of the Olympiad during the 1980 Olympic Games.

In 2012, the Olympic Stadium hosted the European Football Championship. In preparation for this event, the Stadium

ı summer, ***adren-***
line junkies fly
'own the hills
f Protasiv Yar in
zorbas" — trans-
arent inflatable
alls full of air

The slopes are lit up ***every Saturday*** for those who love skiing at night

84

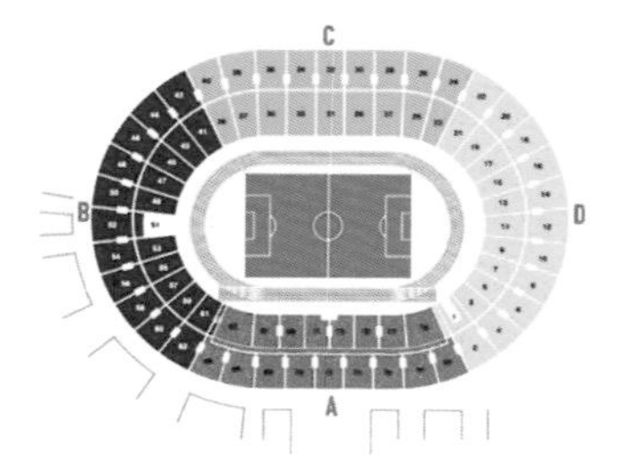

Olympic Stadium

The country's main sports arena sits nestled into one of the central hills in Kyiv

Ukraine's National Sports Complex — the Olympic Stadium — first opened in 1923. In true Soviet form it was called "Red Stadium" at the time. Its fantastic location adds to its atmosphere — it is situated in the centrally located Alekseevskyi Park, near the base of Cherepanova Mountain. The mountain's slopes were utilized in the construction of the stadium's stands. Not long after opening, the Stadium was renovated. Its reopening was going to be celebrated with a Dynamo Kyiv football match on June 22, 1941, until WWII broke out on that very same day. From that day forward, major sporting events would be postponed for years to come.

In 1966 the Stadium was again renovated, and for a time it had the largest capacity of any stadium in the Soviet Union and Europe. Kyiv's Stadium held seven football matches of the Olympiad during the 1980 Olympic Games.

In 2012, the Olympic Stadium hosted the European Football Championship. In preparation for this event, the Stadium

The National Sports Complex "Olympic Stadium" has ***a histor museum*** where you'll find many unique objects — from photograph and sports trophies to items from the private collections of fan

as rebuilt, turning it into a modern arena. Work continued
r almost four years under the supervision of German ar-
itects. A canopy of semi-transparent synthetic membrane
vered spectator seating, protecting onlookers from rain, but
ting the sun through — allowing grass to grow on the field.

Today, the sports complex can hold an impressive crowd of
,000. While the Stadium is known for its football matches,
ack and field competitions and concert events are also held
ere. Madonna, George Michael, Shakira, and bands like
peche Mode and the Red Hot Chili Peppers have all played at
e Stadium. Okean Elzy's performance on June 21, 2014, was
e largest commercial concert in the history of Ukraine.

The complex is massive: *146,000 square meters*. During events, the arena and stands are lit by 608 spotlights

TECHNOLOGY

Right page: Viktor Marushchenko, Mykola Amosov, 1979, Kyiv

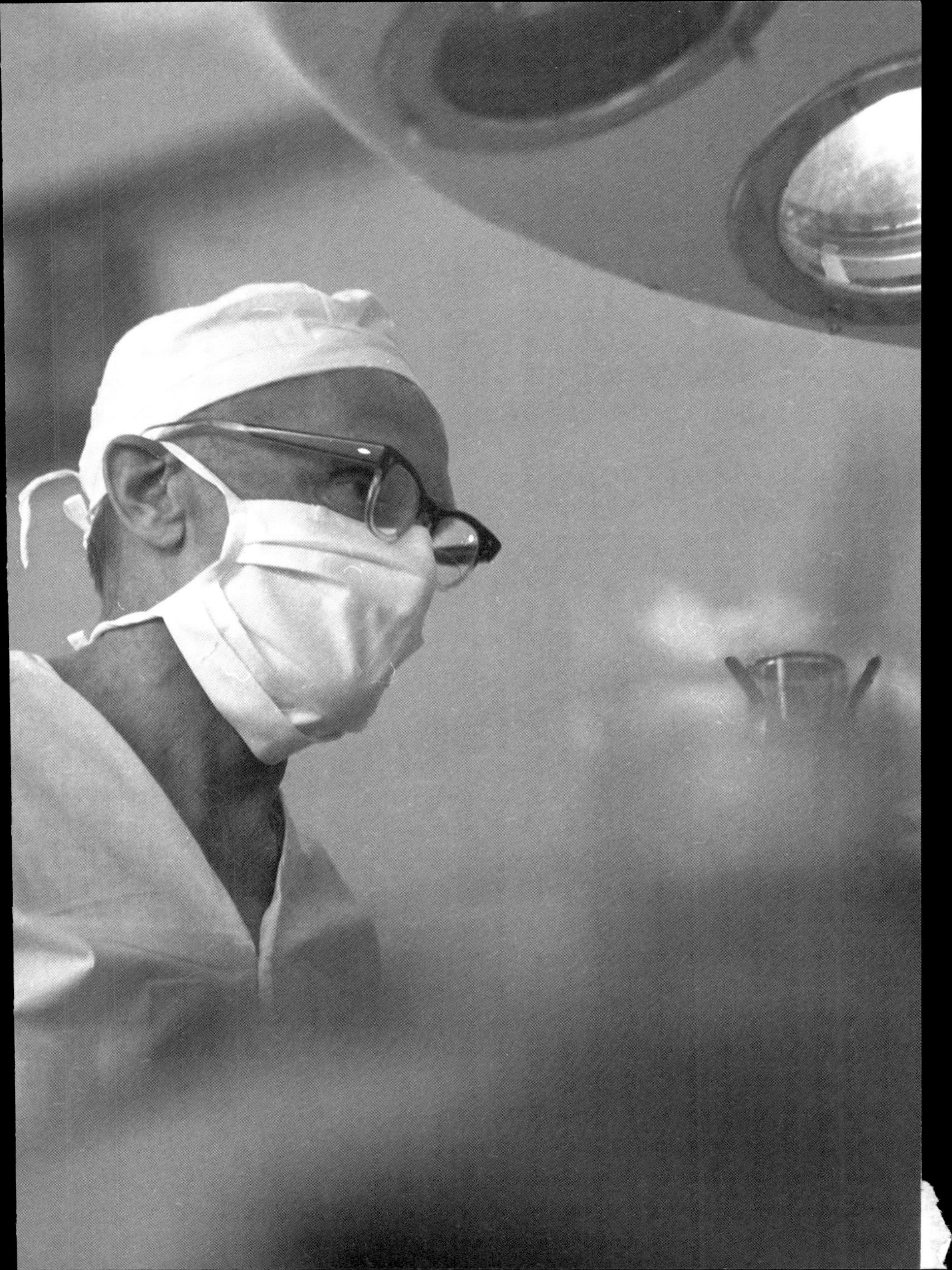

85

Yevhen Paton

Paton's innovative bridge designs have left an indelible mark on Kyiv

Paton was one of the most important scientific minds of the industrial epoch in Ukraine. He pioneered innovations in welding and joining for a variety of purposes, but in Kyiv he is best known for his bridges.

Upon finishing his studies in Dresden and St. Petersburg, the French-born Paton took up research and teaching. The Paton Bridge over the Dnipro is among Paton's most prominent work. It was built in 1953 and was the world's first all-welded bridge. The bridge stretches more than one and a half kilometers in length. Unfortunately, Yevhen Paton neve witnessed its completion — he die three months before the opening of his creation.

Kyiv residents have a special fondness for another of Paton's bridges, the "Lovers' Bridge", across a ravine in Maryinskyi Park. Beyon bridges, Paton's legacy includes 35 scientific papers.

Built in 1941-53, this was ***the world's first all-welded bridge*** and is also the longest bridge in Kyiv, with a length of 1,543 meters

Ihor Sikorskyi

The future designer of the famous amphibious helicopters built his first aircrafts in the backyard of a local Kyiv house

Ihor Sikorskyi was an innovator. He was born in 1889 in to the-family of a Kyiv University professor, and from childhood, he was fond of science and adored the drawings of Leonardo da Vinci. Even as he studied at Kyiv Polytechnical Institute, Ihor started crafting models of helicopters in the field of his father's house at Yaroslaviv Val Street. By 1911, he had set the world flight speed record, piloting an aircraft of his own design.

Ihor Sikorskiy famous hat can be found at his company's museum. Test pilots have adopted the ritual of touchir the hat before test flight

he Sikorsky H-34 is a piston-engine military helicopter used by the US Army

Soon, Sikorskyi designed the world's first multi-engine ircraft, the Russian Champion (the "Grand") and the legend- ry bomber, the Ilya Muromets, becoming becoming a sort of elebrity in the Russian Empire. With the Revolution of 1917, ne designer decided to emigrate. He moved to the United States nd started his own company, the Sikorsky Aircraft Corporation, hich remains a leading aircraft design company to this day.

Ihor Sikorskyi designed several airplanes and helicopters, yet e always considered his greatest achievement to be the inven- on of an amphibious helicopter, which was able to land on ater. This invention has saved the lives of thousands of people ught in natural disasters.

In the Sikorsky Aircraft's first years, the company was saved from bankruptcy by a well-known composer, ***Sergei Rachmaninov.*** He lent Ihor ***$5,000***, a considerable amount of money at that time

87

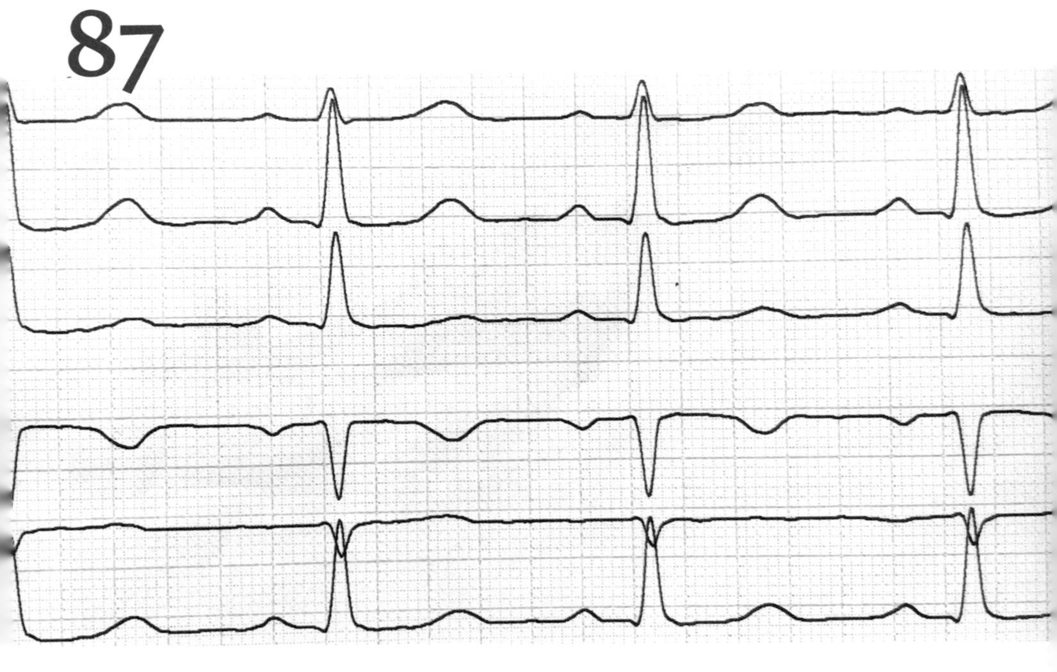

Mykola Amosov

World-renowned heart surgeon, founder of bio cybernetics in Ukraine, and a prolific writer — Amosov's contributions are manifold

Occasionally, solitary geniuses emerge in culture and science, whose ideas and innovations spread throughout the globe. Mykola Amosov is on such individual.

Amosov was born to Russian peasants, fought in the Second World War, and ended up moving to Kyiv to practice medicine in the mid-1960s. With interests bridging medicine and technology, he established new techniques in his field, with particular contributions in the areas of cardi ac surgery and biocybernetics.

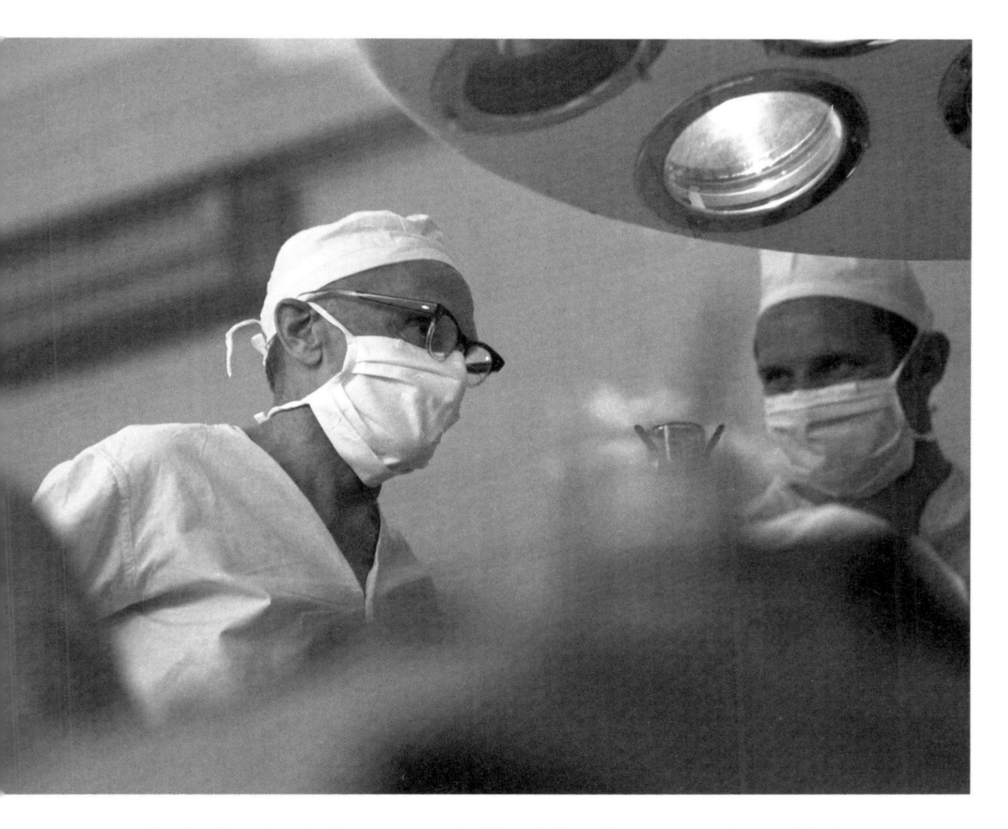

osov was vocal about how hard it was to deal with patient
ths. This was the subject of his first short novel ***Thoughts***
d the Heart *(1967)*

In 2003 the Institute of Cardiovascular Surgery of Ukraine was ***named after Amosov***

Amosov performed more than six thousand heart surgeries, many
them with extracorporeal blood circulation. He was the first person
the USSR to create a mitral valve prosthesis.

Beyond medicine, Amosov dedicated a lot of attention to psycholo-
and sociology. The range of his research was impressive: from ar-
ficial intelligence to the global problems of mankind and matters of
e heart. He authored hundreds of publications, and his contributions
the world of science, technology, and medicine are prolific.

88

The Pivdennyi Bridge

Kyiv is made even more picturesque thanks to its 60 bridges and viaducts — the Pivdennyi (Southern) Bridge is the tallest among them

As a city split in two by the mighty, winding Dnipro, it will come as no surprise that there are a lot of bridges in Kyiv. The first bridge across the Dnipro River was built in the time of Volodymyr Monomakh in 1115. Since that time, bridges and ferries in the city proliferated, yet none of them have lasted very long. Many residents took to crossing the river in winter by foot, a dangerous endeavor. It was only in 1853 that the first stationary bridge across the Dnipro River was built — a stone chain-bridge, named after the emperor of that time, Nikolai I. For a long time, the majestic structure remained the capital's trademark; the bridge opened to let the ships pass, and it bore streetcars But in 1920, during the Soviet-Polish War, the bridge was blown up by Polish troops. Five years after this, its remnants were used to construct a new bridge based on Yevhen Paton design. But, like the others before it it too was destroyed — lasting only until the Second World War. There's now a subway bridge at this locatior

It is thought that Nikolai's chain bridge — whose silver replica was exhibited in London in 1854 — became ***the prototype of the Brooklyn Bridge in New York***

In the 1930s, the Soviet government started building a secret ***tunnel under the Dnipro River*** — an emergency exit out of the city in case of war. But war started too soon. When hostilities began in 1941, its construction was abandoned

The city's tallest bridge, the outhern Bridge, offers great views of ne city from a height of 135 meters. he Southern Bridge is also the short-st route from the city center to Kyiv's nain Boryspil Airport. Built in 1990, was the most modern bridge in ne USSR. The oldest bridges in Kyiv re the Petrivskyi Railroad Bridge pened after reconstruction in 1923) nd the Paton Bridge, built in 1953, hich is also longest at 1,543 meters. ne newest one is the Haven Bridge, built in 2010. The next bridge slated for construction is a two-level Podil bridge, designed to support both car and subway traffic.

Kyiv also has numerous pedestrian bridges. One of the most charming ones is the Lovers' Bridge over a ravine in Maryinskyi Park where couples can "lock" their love to its guardrails. The adventurous can head to Parkovy Pedestrian Bridge (which connects the Right Bank to Trukhaniv Island) to bungee jump.

89

Kyiv Hydroelectric Station

You won't find "Kyiv Sea" written on any maps, but locals regularly descend on this artificial lake, which exists thanks to the dam

It's really just a lake, but locals call it a "sea" because you can't see the other side when you look at it from its bank. This artificial lake on the Dnipro Rive was created in 1964 thanks to the Kyiv Hydroelectric Plant. The area that the government designated to be flooded for this reservoir originally had 300 settlements on it that ended up having to be cleared. The dam's construction flooded a territory of 922 square kilometers on the Dnipro, forever changing the landscape.

The sandy shores scattered along the reservoir seem to invite you to go in and swim; however, ecologists do not recommend that you do so. Firstly, mines and shells from the Second World War that have not yet detonated stil lurk in the reservoir's depths. Secondly, after the Chernobyl Nuclear Power Plant disaster, many radioactive substances — in particular caesium and

Kyiv Hydroelectric Power Station is the first in ***a cascade of hydroelectric power stations*** on the Dnipro River — it's one of six

Kyiv Hydroelectric Power Station is located in ***the city of Vyshhorod***, to the north of Kyiv. It produces about 797 million kilowatt hours of electricity per year, working with an output of 408.5 MW

:rontium — have accumulated at the bottom of the Kyiv Sea. Despite all its eauty, the Kyiv Sea is one of the world's most dangerous structures. Should ıe dam be breached, the whole of Kyiv and the surrounding areas could be ooded. However, scientists affirm that it meets all the safety requirements.

Kyiv Motorcycle Plant

Famous for its rough-terrain motorbikes

The Kyiv Motorcycle Plant is known for its robust and classic bikes and sidecars that you can take on rough terrain. The plant was established in September 26, 1945, on the base of the former armor repair factory.

The first motorcycle off the plant floor was the K-750 — an upgraded version of the famous military motorcycle M-72. The first Dnipro brand motorcycle was the MT-10, launched in 1974.

The plant has produced escort motorcycles since 1976. Two years after production began, a lot of 25 specialized escort motorcycles for the Kremlin were manufactured. The high-quality, powerful and reliable vehicles made them a favorite of bodyguards for the Soviet elite. At fifty horsepower strong and with special tires, this motorcycle could maintain a speed of up to 130 kph on a slippery road — even in winter. Thanks to its electric starter, you can count on the engine to keep running, even at temperatures of -40°C.

Today, the Kyiv Motorcycling Plant continues its tradition of metalworking expertise — blacksmithing, casting, and heat treatment—with a variety of models and also custom work.

These motorcycles have been featured in several films — ***Indiana Jones*** among them!

Some ***1.5 million Dnipro*** machines were built for the armed forces of the USSR

Engineers of the Kyiv Motorcycle Plant working on an experimental high-speed motorbike

91

UNIT.City

Ukraine's first innovation park

UNIT.City is location where a top infrastructure and an all-inclusive business ecology, innovative and creative businesses get themselves set up. The mission of UNIT.City is to create a unique innovation platform where advanced companies, start-ups and lone entrepreneurs can cross paths and get together to inspire growth and promote better-quality business.

By 2020 UNIT.Ci strives to becor ***a one-point entry*** into Ukrai for investors, businesses and new technology from all over the world

UNIT.City dedicates special attention to education and related activities. One of the critical elements of its ecosystem is the UNIT Factory coding school that uses a

utting-edge curriculum designed by French School 42. On op of the education facilities, UNIT.City provides space for ectures, meet-ups and conferences.

The tech park offers its residents a package of additional ervices for business development: assistance in commer-ialization and fundraising, counseling and legal services, oaching, mentoring and accelerating programs, prototyp-ng laboratories, and more. In this context, the park engages nternational partnership with global technology compa-ies, venture capital funds, business associations, leading ducational institutions, and innovation hubs.

Besides business infrastructure, UNIT.City will also include a smaller residential district to complete the comfortable environment of the tech park, making it ***a place to work and live***

92